Original
Poems

Original Poems

LLOYD ANDRESEN

iUniverse

ORIGINAL POEMS

iUniverse books may be ordered through booksellers or by contacting:

iUniverse
1663 Liberty Drive
Bloomington, IN 47403
www.iuniverse.com
1-800-Authors (1-800-288-4677)

Because of the dynamic nature of the Internet, any web addresses or links contained in this book may have changed since publication and may no longer be valid. The views expressed in this work are solely those of the author and do not necessarily reflect the views of the publisher, and the publisher hereby disclaims any responsibility for them.

Any people depicted in stock imagery provided by Getty Images are models, and such images are being used for illustrative purposes only. Certain stock imagery © Getty Images.

ISBN: 978-1-5320-6969-7 (sc)
ISBN: 978-1-5320-6970-3 (e)

Print information available on the last page.

iUniverse rev. date: 04/05/2019

A Place That's Rare

With computer ready, and mouse in hand
The virtual world, is at my command
I 'surf the net', for a place that's 'hip'
Somewhere to take my annual trip

England, cavorting with ladies and Earls
Or Hawaii, diving for trinkets and pearls
To France, seeing the Lido Review
Or tasting wines like, Chablis or Anjou

See the Paris sites, and I'd have a blast
From every bar, I'd be the last...
The grandest dream of mortal man
"Tripping the life" ...Then, again

Do I want to hang with
the beautiful crowd
Strutting around, haughty and proud?
Where pretense, is the only game
And nothing is real — What a shame

Oh, to find a place that's rare
Breathing fresh, unsoiled air
A beautiful land, that's worlds apart
To find yourself, and lose your heart

A secluded spot, off the 'beaten path'
Perhaps go somewhere, few men hath
To frolic in the morning dew
In a place like Fez or Timbuktu

I think I'll visit Africa
Though not Camelot or Shangri-La

It has a rustic ambiance
No bottled water or croissants

A land where man and beast roam free
In Mother Nature's vast menagerie
Sights and sounds, I've never heard
A cheetah or secretary bird

Although, the trip is danger fraught
I am, at heart, an Argonaut
I'll gird my loins, and watch my back
Perhaps, a knife or gun, I'll pack

A beast, I hope, I don't adjoin
And become a lion's tenderloin
Or be bitten, by a snake
What a mark, that would make!

Notwithstanding, trial or peril
This ancient land, pristine and feral
Exudes with charm and comeliness
Friendly people, too, I'd guess

Folks who toil and abide
In a world, where no walls divide
They coexist with the beast
And seem to hold their own, at least

Life is harsh, out on the plain
Think I'll see it all by train
Africa — I misgive
A nice place to see, but not to live

Lover's Tale

Captivated by your charm
Your light and winsome manner
My longing heart, told me, dear
You'd fill my weekly planner

I placed you on a pedestal
And viewed your lovely face
You were my fair and radiant queen
I bowed to you, your grace

All I could, I'd do for you
While playing the cavalier
I was your champion, Lancelot
You...my Guinevere

I was living in a fantasy world
My mind was overtaken-
By the sweet perfume, of passion's breath
If this be dream, let me not awaken

But, as time went by, you changed
And doubt began to fester
The less, your gallant prince, I felt
The more, your humble jester

Your indifference, puzzled me
And I questioned your sincerity
Was this love, I thought we shared
Merely, a vicious parody?

The love and warmth, I gave to you
I felt it not returning
Your apathy left a pungent scent
As a bridge, when it starts burning

Once, my dear, I believed in you
Fervently, I did so
In my heart, a special love
That, on you, I did bestow

It hurts me now, to realize
That I was but a pawn
I see you in a different light
No more, a gentle fawn

Instead, this woman, you have become
Is so very hard and callous
A vitriolic entity
Full of bitterness and malice

Dear, indeed, you broke my heart
Into a million shards
Tearing at my very soul
And the fragile man, it guards

Still, I'd take you back, today
If you'd only say the word
I would even take the blame
For all that has occurred

There are some, who'd call me mad
For thinking as I do
But no one knows, just how I feel
They haven't got a clue

If I'd put my motives, into verse
They would surely sound absurd
So I'll keep them to myself
Ne'er utter a single word

I will say, to those who scorn
And fail to comprehend
Instead of criticizing me
This, I recommend

Look into a lover's heart
And here's what you will find
That what the poets say, is so
Love, is truly blind

An Ego, Altered

My newest friend, is an angle worm
I found atop an earthen berm
A worm, as a pet?
Must be kismet
...Think I'll call him, Herm

Herm was cool, but just for kicks
I taught him to do some party tricks
A silly hat
And things like that
That I brought into the mix

My friends would holler and hoot
And say to each other, "how cute"
But with hat removed
They disapproved
Not knowing which end to salute

We'd perform for the local gentry
They'd never fail, to bid us entry
We'd grab our portion
Of fame and fortune
The rest, would be elementary

Soon, we got our first gig
At the request, of some country bigwig
The stage was now set
For this unlikely duet
Now, from the cup of success, we'd swig

This was our big chance
For glory and romance
We could be famous

Like 'Andy and Amos'
As we'd work the old 'song and dance'

The seed had now been sewn
I was really in a zone
But Herm, seemed unwilling
To make a 'killing'
For alas, he had no backbone

I was angry, and I was hurt-
That he was becoming an introvert
In lieu of consuming
The fruit of life, at its blooming
Herm would rather eat dirt

At that moment, I realized
I'd become the one thing I despised
A self-centered heel
Unable to feel-
The pain of a friend, utilized

I knew what I must do
He needed a change of venue
To friendly terrain
And ever remain
'Til life bids him, adieu

As for me, I'll get by
Though a tear, oft stain my eye
Recalling the term
I had with Herm
My partner — my friend — my ally

Streets of Shame

I've walked these streets, a million times
And faced the great unknown
Though, surrounded by the crowd
I feel so all alone

Another day, I've survived
And gained my 'daily bread'
And though, I'm still on this earth
I fear what lies ahead

Every day is much the same
Among my social caste
Though each new day, is like the first
Each night, could be my last

Living in a world of fear
Never knowing who to trust
Self-esteem has given way
To abasement and disgust

Shadowed figures, fill my life
The brigands and the whores
People filled with broken dreams
That society ignores

Ever living on the 'edge'
I pause to catch my breath
Pimps and dealers, everywhere
Selling ecstasy and meth

Another victim claimed, today
A young girl, in her teens

Pulled into this dreadful life
For, she had no other means

I muse, if I will end like her
Face-down, in the slime
Supply the final sacrifice
Cut down in my prime

Would anybody mourn my death?
Or would they scowl and say,
"Another vermin, 'bit the dust'
Who needs them, anyway"?

Or will I live, and not yet see
The backseat of a hearse?
I'm not really sure, at all
Which scenario is worse

Why won't someone rescue me?
From this living hell
Save me from impending doom
In this place, where demons dwell

I feel, my most fervent prayers
Have fallen on deaf ears
How can you, my God, ignore
Your servant's abject tears

Perhaps the fate, of one like me
Is sealed, and can't be varied
Doomed to roam these morbid streets
Until I'm dead and buried

In tomorrow's backstreet news
Pages from the lead
You may find some tragic lines
And this is how they'll read:

"Another victim claimed today
Only twenty-three
Taken much too soon"
Perhaps, it will be me

Final Destination

"One by one, two by twos
Round up all the bastard Jews
Why, you ask...l don't know
Because the Fuehrer told me so"

"We need to meet our quota, men
One thousand Jews; tomorrow, ten
These people are a great disgrace
Must preserve the master race- a

Said the brazen Nazi thugs
No time left for farewell hugs
"Jews, you must come with us, now
Leave your sickle, and your plow"

And so, the genocide's begun
What's started now, can't be undone
The cries of several generations
Will resonate, through all the nations

Driven from their homes and shops
It seems as though, it never stops
Take one Jew, then another
Everyone, and his brother

Put them on a bus or train
Must amass, and detain
Never tell them, where they're going
Let their pangs of fear, keep growing

The final destination site
Debarking in the dim half-light

Led into a world of gloom
For many, it will be their doom

Nothing much to eat or drink
Memories, their only link-
To a life, they used to know
Come what may, they can't let go

Some will die, some will not
Victims of the hangman's knot
Broken bodies, in the oven
Of the vicious Nazi coven

Not only Jews, felt the sting
But others, worth remembering
The lame, the weak, the indigent
For all of these, we still lament

The remnant, can bear witness to
The horrid things, that man can do
If chaos is the only law-
We're living in a world of straw

Though some, I feel, knew it wrong
But feeling threatened, by the throng
Carried out the Devil's plot
To seal for e'er, the Jewish lot

Yesterday, you knew them well
Today, they're in a living hell Justify?
You simply can't...
The ramblings of a tyrant's rant

The lessons, which we should have learned
Have been ignored, and roundly spurned
If we cannot feel aghast-
Then we are doomed, to repeat the past

It's started now, in many lands
To abolish some, by other's hands
I fear, the worst, is yet to come
And the very thought, leaves me numb

What the future of man will hold
By the ancients, has been told
If the final niche of man is hewn
Then bring the rapture, and bring it soon

Contents

Everlasting Love

Of all the flowers, on God's green earth
I believe, the one He chose
To display beauty, for all its worth
Is the frail, yet lovely rose

My dear, I give this rose to you
That smells so very sweet
As a symbol, that my heart is true
And with love, it is replete

A love, not borne of a carnal ideal
To rise, and then decline
Rather, one that is completely real
And will stand the 'test of time'

A time, not measured in human mortality
Nor, the seconds on a dial
But endless - Without finality
As wind, o'er a distant isle

A space apart, where we can live
And love, until we die
Then, ambrosial blooms to you, I'll give
From our 'island' in the sky

A Brief Encounter

I met a girl in Monterrey
Below the Rio Grande
A woman to fulfill my dreams
Amid the cactus and the sand

She was only thirty-one
l, a score her elder
Yet, my eager heart, leapt in me
The moment I beheld her

The body of a goddess?- No
But slender and petite
Though, I doubt if Aphrodite
Had a smile, so warm and sweet

Silky hair, black as night
And flashing eyes, to match
That shimmered 'neath the waxing moon
As its golden beams, they'd catch

Her skin was smooth, and blemish free
With a slightly brownish hue
I felt, my will, was not my own
The nearer that I drew

Her face — that face, was heavenly
Of her, I was in awe
I looked at her, as one in love
My stare, I could not withdraw

She smiled at me, then touched my arm
And I was swept away
Amidst a sea of wonderment
I'll ne'er forget that day

Her hand, she gave so willingly
It was all that I could do-
To keep emotions, that I felt
Within, and out of view

Her allure, ne'er gave my heart
A single moment's rest
It was truly magical
The charm that she possessed

Behold! This vision of loveliness
Wrapped in 'golden chain'
I loved her as a man obsessed
But alas, it was in vain

'l cherish our time together"
She told me, with a pout
'l love you like no other
Of that, there is no doubt"

"But this night, my heart is heavy-laden
Filled with sorrow, and with pain
You'll be ever in my dreams
But what I must do, is plain"

She told of how, she was not free
To accept my yearning heart
Her story, sent a chill through me
And tore my world apart

Her love, to me, she could not give-
And be another's wife
Feeling that she could not assume
And sustain, this double life

There were hugs, and many tears
(Emotions on display)
Then, she gently kissed my cheek
Turned, and walked away

Now, I'm left with memories
And yes, there is regret-
Of a love I had, then lost
I mourn for her— And yet-

Somehow, I feel an inner peace
Though, this bridge, I now must burn
Content, that I once gave my love
And WAS loved in return

Wind Beneath My Wings

Words of praise were sent my way
From relatives and friends
Niceties, they all display
Then, reality descends

If truth be told
I'm not the man you married years ago
At times, I was aloof and cold
And belligerent...l know

But through it all, you stood by me
Steadfastly, all the while
You had the chance to bolt and flee
But that, dear, was not your style

You were the wind beneath my wings
The strength, I never had
Eternal love — How true it rings
But I was blind — So sad

I failed to say, how much I cared
(I wish I had a penny) —
For every time, those words were spared
Dear, there were so many

Seldom, would you rule the day
Mostly doing what I'd choose
But darling, now I'm here to say —
You've overpaid your dues

Whenever I'd be feeling stressed
And things were getting tough —
A gentle kiss...a warm caress

When words, just weren't enough

Dear, you always had the 'smarts'
While I was mediocre
Oh, my precious queen of hearts —
How could you love this joker?

You'd stretch a dollar, 'til it bled
Then make it bleed, again
So we could buy our 'daily bread'
Thank God for you...amen

The wolf was never at our door
You always saw to that
Every day, another chore
Each day, a different hat

My lovely one, you were the glue
That held this family, fast
The memories I have of you...
Forever, will they last

For now, my dear, the poem is through
This tale of love and glory
Tomorrow, I may start anew
For, it's a never-ending story

Rest

Dear, I stand here by your side
With feelings, unexpressed
It's been a long day, I know
So rest, my lovely - Rest
I kiss your cheek, I hold your hand
My passion, I can't arrest
Someday we'll talk, but as for now
Rest, my lady - Rest
Your fair name, I softly speak
Of its beauty, I've oft professed
I long to hold you, but you must
Rest, my sweetness - Rest
Many friends, we met today
Here, not by request
The receiving is done, your labors are through
Just rest, my darling - Rest
The crowd is gone, all is still
Save, this pounding in my chest
It's waning now, I feel content
Ever rest, my angel — Rest

Unrequited Love

It's hard to write these lines to you
Sobbing all the while
With copious tears, I can't subdue
This is my 'hour of trial'

I realize, that we can never be
I knew it from the start
My eyes were just too blind to see
The pain within your heart

Not wanting to harm my self-esteem
You struggled with your sanity
I'd keep pushing you to the extreme
Just to stroke my vanity

I was wrong, I now see
To try and win your heart
That's not the way, you wanted me
There was no desire, on your part

If a love is unrequited
Fruit, it can never bear
If into both hearts, it's not invited
Contentment, can hardly be there

My intentions now, are more benign
No longer, do I yearn
I now have no design —
On your heart, and in return —

I won't expect more from you
Than heart-felt cordiality
One thing I've learned, and this is true
A lesson in stark reality

I still want to be your friend, you see
In good times, and in bad
I pray, someday, you'll say to me —
"You're the best friend, I ever had"

A Friend-Indeed

My friend, I'll ever love you
The rest of my natural days
You've touched my life, o cherished one
In so many wondrous ways

For the sake of brevity, my dear
I'll hint at but a few
Yet, they must ever capture
The very essence of you

A smile—a kind word
Are two, toward which I'm leaning
Bound together, with a kiss
To punctuate their meaning

With every smile, you flash my way
(Your countenance brightly beaming)
My heart and mind, they do imbue
And send my senses screaming

As a Cheshire Cat...that imposing grin
Hypnotic, to say the least
Upon its mesmerizing charm-
My mind's eye, will forever feast

With gentle words, aptly placed
You build my self-esteem
Those of encouragement, solace and more
Will fulfill my most impossible dream

That I could have a friend like you —
On whom I can rely-
When life is pleasant, and when it's not
Compassion, you personify

Exuding warmth where e're you go
Never donning a persona
Peace and joy, you also afford
Like a benevolent Madonna

Another gift you give me, dear
That gives my heart a tug
With outstretched arms, you reach for me
Then, grace me with a hug

A hug is not a panacea
In fact, it's hardly needed
But I wouldn't trade it, for the world
When my confidence has receded

I pray, this bond 'tween you and me
Never breaks, though it has been stretched
You're always in my reverie
On my mind — firmly etched

Our love is of a special kind
Chaste, and wholly platonic
An affinity, seldom seen
Reserved, yet extremely harmonic

The memories within my heart
(Whether graphic or subtleties)
Waft ever softly, through my mind
As a warm and gentle breeze

It soothes me so, to think of you
My very soul's refreshed
I'm feeling peace, just knowing that
Our hearts are forever meshed

My friend, when e'er the end is near
And around me, angels hover
I'll utter with my dying breath
"She's my friend, and I dearly love her"

Starlight

Few things in life, are inherently ours
A notable exception, the wandering stars
Throughout the dome, God interspersed
The stars — so the darkness won't be cursed

We follow their course, through the great expanse
Our world below, they do enhance
We hold these 'bodies' in great esteem
As sources of wonder, beauty and dream

Though most are impressed, by these beaming pulsation
To young lovers, they convey special connotations
Seen not merely, as lamps in the skies
But as twinkling reflections, in their loved one's eyes

Crystals of light, shimmering above
What an awesome sight, are these luminaries of love
Our passions, they tend to expedite
As everyone knows, love blooms at night

Though simply masses, of searing radiation
We marvel at these spheres of conflagration
These relentless sentinels, that extend such beauty
Enlighten our lives, for that is their duty

Seeing The Light

I recall, that in my formative years
Religion was 'hit or miss'
Though, I enjoyed more joy than fear
Still, I was mired in the abyss-

Of greed, anger, doubt and contention
And I was increasingly wearing a frown
What I needed, was some
divine intervention
Or, in a sea of self-pity, I would drown

It came in the form, of a
charming young girl
Whose comeliness, I could plainly see
Her complexion was that of a creamy pearl
Then, she displayed her
inner beauty, to me

The Lord, was a huge part of her world
A world, I was about to enter
She came to me, with soul unfurled
And I was very glad, He sent her

She taught me things, I'd
not practiced much
Niceties, I had taken for granted
Like a kind word, a gentle touch
My viewpoint was severely slanted

I've always been a compassionate man
In goodwill, I did revel
Though, I'll ever do the best I can
She's taken me to another level

I had never been this way before
My heart and mind, in sync
Like a bumbling knight, in days of yore
In my 'armor', there was a chink

There were areas of my existence
That needed an overhaul
If I didn't receive a spiritual assistance
I'd never hear my 'call'

I've now resolved, to make my mark
In the world, by doing good
Enter the light - reject the dark
And live as Jesus would

Where there is need, I'll lend a hand
From showing mercy, I'll never balk
Patience and prudence...at my command
When I initiate my 'love walk'

Wanting naught, for each noble gesture
Of tenderness and charity
Humility, will be my vesture
With the World - Solidarity

I'll dedicate my life, to charitable deeds
And to nothing untoward
Knowing I've fulfilled other's needs
Will be its own reward

Ode To Cloud

There is nothing peaceful as a cloud
Floating by, noble and proud
With names like cirrus, stratus and cumulus
They brighten our day — they humor us

Coming in various shapes and sizes
And all manner, of funny disguises
Anything your mind can ponder
As through the azure sky, they wander

Some are flat; some round and puffy
With serrated edges that look rather scruffy
Wisps of cotton, against the firmament
Quickly dispersed — Not at all permanent

Here today, gone tomorrow
The best things in life, we only borrow
Images in white, of the Lord's designing
Comely — And replete with a silver lining

Ode To Kitten

By wise men, it has been written
One look, and you'll be smitten
For joy so rare
Naught can compare
With a warm and downy kitten

I may be a feline doter
A boring and obsessive gloater
But this much is clear
Your woes disappear
When they rev up their cute, little 'motor'

The feeling can be alluring
Hearing a tiny kitten purring
You'd be devoid of all senses
If, when this tone commences
The passion in you, is not stirring

A kitten, so helpless and small
Still has the wherewithal-
To send a gloomy disposition
Into a state of remission
Depression, to forestall

Of a cat's therapeutic worth
It's known throughout the earth
Your malady, it's cloaking
When a cat, you are stroking
For, it evokes contentment and mirth

So, the next time you feel a bit flat
And alone in your habitat
Before your nerves go snap Put a cat on your lap
Finding happiness, 'cause that's where it's at

Common Thread

Our friends said It would never last
We're contrary...not the same
At the slightest sign of trouble
We'd fall apart, they'd claim

Family, too, did not approve
They made that very clear
A common theme, they all endorsed
From this union, we must steer

Over time we'd realize
For each other, we were not meant
Best to break it off, right now
Before our lives are spent

Despite their mean and vicious talk
We managed to survive
We dodged their slings and arrows
And all else, they'd contrive

There have been some trying times
When we've been on the 'brink'
But through it all...one common thread
They call it love — l think

A fervent love overlooks-
Your partner's faults and quirks
We've found the way to coexist
And this is how it works:

If one would cleave the other's skin
With a careless word or act
We'd cauterize and bind the wounds
With tenderness and tact

When one of us is overwhelmed
With a pain, that they have carried
The other's cares, are put on hold
It's a given, and never varied

There were times, we both were right
When our egos, would contrast
But compromise, is the 'glue'
That holds a marriage, fast

We will always work it out
However long it may take
'Til the collective windows of our minds
Are clear, and not opaque

Yes, we've silenced all our critics
Left them in the dust
With our shows of dedication
Fidelity and trust

Love is never nine to five
But an overtime endeavor
With a hefty bonus, at the end
To retire with love, forever

Ode To A Muse

When e'er I pen a lovely thought
With every word I choose
My fecund mind is ever fraught
With the essence of my muse
She is my drive and determination
In all things great and small
From her, I get my inspiration
She's ever at my 'beck and call'

If I write about a feisty dame
Or a lovely lady of merit
To me, my friend, they're both the same
Whichever hat I choose, she can wear it
When I'm troubled by an arduous verse
Where nothing seems to fit
And I may rant and rail and curse
But can make no sense of it-

She's always there, to aid my plight
When I want to cease and end it
It's then, she emits her radiant light
To my heart and mind, she sends it
A wispy countenance, does she impart
Yet, classic and well defined
With more compassion in her heart
Than you and l, combined

How can so much love be enwrapped
In such a frail and diminutive torso
At the flash of a smile, it
becomes uncapped
As a spewing geyser - even more so
At times, the muse of poetic love

The nature of which, she embraces
It flows through her, from God above
That's one of her many faces

She personifies regal beauty and charm
As the goddesses of Grecian tales
With these qualities, she tends to disarm
The distaff, as well as the males

This bard, I swear, she does imbue
To the point of saturation
Because of her, it is my view
The sky is the limitation
I could be the greatest poet
The world has ever known
I've been blessed, and I know it
But I couldn't do it alone

I'll need a well, from which to draw
When mine is running dry
And buoy up this man of straw
To give it one more try
If I finally reach the pinnacle
And receive every accolade
I will wax analytical
And put my muse on parade

I'll explain every facet, of this one
Who stimulates my mind
And helps me form a rhyme or pun
That makes me sound refined
When I conclude my dissertation

The world will know my story
I will say, with due mortification
'I cannot take all the glory"

She has been the catalyst
Throughout my brief career
She'd be at the top - (If I had a list)
Of the people, I hold dear
Heaven help me, if I ever lost her
This bard would become obtuse
Though memories of her, I'll ever foster
I could not rhyme without my muse

So here's to you, my genial cohort
My confidant - My friend
Together, we can 'hold the fort'
My muse and l, 'til the end

Madonna

I'd like to quote, if I may
From some long-forgotten bard
It may help to cheer your day
When you've worked so very hard

I give this little verse to you
I rue, I did not write
But dear, it is so very true
I swear, with all my might

"l love you not for what you are
But for what I become,
when I am with you"
These are truer words, by far
Than I can ever give you

I now see you in a different light
Than I ever have, before
Let me tell you, if I might
How it's opened up a door

A door revealing many winders
For one's eyes, to plainly view
It exposes our previous blunders
Of which, dear, I've made a few

I used to see your lovely smile
And other things, neglect
But now, my dear, I've changed my style
I see your intellect

More than just a pretty face
You're sensitive and deep
Humility, you embrace
Virtue, you always keep

Dear, we've bridged many a span
Over the past few years
And I'll remember, as long as I can
Through laughter and through tears-

The foundations we laid
The words that were spoken
The plans that were stayed
Will serve as an unbroken-

Bond between two
Very good friends
Just me and you
Right to the ends-

Of earth and sea
My dear, as we know it
It always will be
The Madonna and the poet

Bittersweet

When it all began, I do not know
Or why I was smitten, so
Perhaps, it was your winning style
That warmed my heart, and made it smile

Dear, you took me quite by storm
Your attentions, kept my vanity warm
Every glance, an ego-trip
That tended to make my propriety slip

Your figure, too, I could not ignore
As every curve, I did explore
Although, I knew it wrong to stare
I only looked, because it was there

In my eyes, there was never lust
Just an ample sprinkling of stardust
It clouds my sight— dear, I am finding
And nearly forgot, whose
store I was minding

Once in a while, my mind goes numb
To my obsession, I do succumb
At times, the things I say and do
Are subject to a full review

Perhaps I gave you the wrong impression
My forte has never been discretion
But I've always loved you, as a friend
It's the only message, I've tried to send

Though, I cannot bear all the blame
If e'er our friendship goes down in flame
Dear, you have so many moods
The sources of which, me, eludes

Talking to you, became a chore
Never knowing, what was in store
Would you be cordial, or berate me?
I'd muse to myself, "what
will her state be"?

You're soft and gentle, then turn on a dime
Seemingly, without reason or rhyme
It's frightening, how you vacillate
From Jekyll to Hyde, you alternate

At times, I'd become disenchanted
And my allegiance...recanted
But then, you'd use your copious charm
And my ruffled demeanor, totally disarm

Eventually, we'd reconcile
And all would be great —for awhile
We'd try to make it, but alas
A rift would always come to pass

I'd inform you of my benign intent
But you'd think my claims, fraudulent
Dear, I was not your adversary
Though, you found my
remarks, quite contrary

If I said white, you'd think it black
Of perception, there was a lack
If we can never become in sync
From the cup of suspicion,
        we'll forever drink

Dear, you thought my heart, untrue
Not meaning the words, I'd say to you
Never knowing if you could fully trust
This man that fate, had upon you, thrust

I tell you now, each word was meant
From nary a one, will I repent?
I tell the truth...I always have
Honesty, is a healing salve

At times, I know the truth can hurt
But, misunderstandings, it can avert
Its better, your ego be disarranged
Than your mind be unyielding,
        and never changed

There are some, who think
        me quite insane
Returning to you, again and again
Leave her be — she doesn't care
Wash your hands, of the whole affair"

They may be right, in what they say
But my wistful heart, I must obey
I can't forsake this relationship
Though, on my emotions,
        I must get a grip

I'll be a remorseful penitent
For the 'common good', I will relent
The longer...in the present vein
The more, this man, you will disdain

To keep you as a friend, indeed
The 'writing-on-the-wall', I will heed
Every nuance, I will discern
Lest this friendship, 'crash and burn'

Is this affinity a fairyland?
Ever shifting, as grains of sand?
Or can it survive, and even flourish
If with love and patience, it, we nourish?

I pray, that we can work things out
Nevermore, to rail and shout
With God's blessing, and loving Grace
We will endure, and finish the race

What Goes Around...

It's true, you were my shining star
And quickly stole my heart
Then like a virtual scimitar
You rent it all apart

Don't tell me, you played around —
And simply say, "I'm sorry"
Well, I'm not swayed, by the sound
Of your passion-filled sob story

You want me to take you back
So you can feel absolved
And not expect to take some flak —
For how it's all evolved

And I'm to hail your return
And not be sad or bitter
It's time, my dear, that you learn
I'm not your baby sitter

You're guilty of the gravest sin
A woman can commit
Each excuse, is wearing thin
They never seem to quit

I can't return my heart to you —
Remove it from the shelf
And wonder if you will be true
When you don't know, yourself

To forgive and forget —
Is Heavenly, they say
But each day, by hell, I am beset
Please, just go away

I'm not your puppet, on a string
Good-bye for now, you're free
May you enjoy a wanton fling
It just won't be with me

A 'Tail' of Love

A canine, is man's best friend
Or so the adage goes
He'll never judge, or condescend
His fidelity, ever grows

You can yell, and give a dog
A hearty reprimand
He'll absorb your stinging monologue
Then, gently lick your hand

Rex, Spike, Jack or King
What e'er the nomenclature
For man, he will do anything
As truly, that is his nature

His capacity to love-
No one can ever question
He will follow, anywhere
At the least suggestion

If you're walking down a darkened street
And he lets out a growl
It behooves, not to be indiscreet
Perhaps, danger's on the prowl

If you find, that no one's there
Try not to hurt his pride
He thought it best, to balk and stare
Than not, and let it slide

Fervent love and gratitude
Is all that he desires
He's not uncommonly courtly or shrewd
But he'll serve, 'til he expires

I wish that folks, would act the same
(Being so inclined)
Never curse or chide or blame
And repay all love, in kind

'Til that scenario comes about
Here's the message, that I send
Of his devotion, there is no doubt
A dog, is man's best friend

Awe-Struck

Once, I held you in esteem
By you, I was inspired
My imagination's catalyst
And the spark, by which it's fired

I longed to be just like you
In every way I could
That you had led the perfect life
Was fully understood

If anyone would 'put you down'
I was sure of their intent
It was only jealousy
Surely, self-evident

I had long convinced myself-
There was nothing to those claims
Only folks with evil minds-
Would play such hurtful games

But the more I'd hear, their searing words-
Toward the man that I admire-
Even you, my friend
That trite expression came to mind-
'Where there's smoke, there's fire'

If there was but a hint of truth-
In anything that they said-
I would look the classic fool
For you, I had misread

I would look 'neath every rock
Each tree, I'd peer behind
Advancing apprehensively
Afraid what I might find

Was your 'sainthood' premature?
Had my trust been all in vain?
Trying to ignore each charge
Did naught, to ease my pain

If nothing's found, to prove them wrong
How little consolation
For doubt will haunt me everyday
Of my life, for its duration

Perhaps it's best, I never know
About those scathing accusations
Shady business deals
Or extra-marital relations

If they're true, or if they're not
Is the point, no more
Rather, my 'blind faith' policy
That I now deplore

I guess, we all have our faults
Even you my friend
Into the pit of negligence
We all, at times, descend

Though, I resolve from this point, on
To keep an open mind
See the world, with candid eyes
Not with ones so blind

In you, I'll keep believing
My faith, I won't withdraw
I'll look at you with amity
But never again, with awe

The Prodigal Friend

I know you're angry with the world
(A dangerous frame of mind)
It pains me so, to see a friend
Walking around half-blind

You only see the tawdry side
And you tell me, "this is real"
Where people think, it is their right
To lie and cheat and steal

You say, you want to join the crowd
Taste the good life, while in supply
Be completely on your own
On no one else, rely—

Save, a few bawdy friends
Who may be gone tomorrow?
Rob you of your honor...
Your friendship, only borrow

I don't mean, to paint a scene
Of ceaseless 'doom and gloom'
Just open up your heart and mind —
To my words — while there's still room

I'm not saying that you must conform
And to everyone, be a blessing
But don't make a choice,
then close the door
Leave room for 'second-guessing'

Prudence, is a worthy tool
Always keep it near

It can save you from an early grave
When exploring a new frontier

But, arrogance destroys the soul
Don't let it be your master
Excessive pride and animosity
Is a formula for disaster

In the world, there must be compromise
It does not owe you a living
If you want your share, of its respect
In return, what are you giving?

So try and keep a balance
Never going to extremes
My friend, this is the only way
To realize your dreams

I'm not trying to preach to you
Just giving you sound advice
Before moving on, ask yourse
If Is it worth the sacrifice?

Though, if you must try your wings
Don't leave all else behind
Those 'chains' you said,
would hold you down
May be the 'ties that bind'

Whatever you decide to do
This, I underscore
I'll always be here for you
Because, that's what friends are for

Maintaining Amity

At first, my actions did contain
Elements, I found hard to explain
Ever playing the boor
I'd keep pushing for more
I knew not, the meaning of 'maintain'

At times, I'd transgress your domain
Acting obnoxious and inane
While trying to earn an edge
Between us, I was driving a wedge
I had not yet learned to 'maintain'

I must preserve all that I gain
Every triumph, I do attain
From this one I adore-
I will receive even more
If I will only resolve to 'maintain'

Now, the gauntlet, to me, is lain
My vanity, I must enchain
Take my heart, as a token
Of a bond, never broken
And a friendship, I'll ever
work to 'maintain'

The writing on the wall is plain
This charade, I cannot sustain
I'll now take what is given
By amity, I'll be driven
Above all, I must 'maintain'

The demons of obsession, are slain
Nevermore, to establish their reign

Now, restraint is patrolling
And my heart, it's controlling
I'm learning, my dear, to 'maintain'

For your favors, to retain
From contention, I will refrain
Softly I'll tread
Lest I break this common thread
That I try so hard, to 'maintain'

No liberties did I take - profane
Ever trying to act humane
Leaving my vanity behind
To humility, I am resigned
This friendship, I ever vow to 'maintain'

Upon my character, there is a stain
And ever will it remain
Unless I can atone
For the foul seeds, I have sewn
And keep firm, my pledge, to 'maintain'

Now that obsession, is on the wane
I must assume, a more modest vein
Anything less
And I may regress
So, it will behoove me, to 'maintain'

Throughout this whole campaign
One thing has been germane
A commitment to accord
And the niceties, it does afford
This love, we must ever 'maintain

The Maturation of Sarah

She wears the crown of womanhood
Upon the braids of a child
The embodiment, of all that is good
So young and undefiled

Yesterday, a babe-in-arms
Oh, how the years steal by
Today, replete with a woman's charms
Delicate, yet, pleasing to the eye

This little girl, is coming of age
A budding debutante
My winsome smile, belies my rage
My eyes, are a billowing font

These tears, my friend, will never wane
They will merely change position
Through my heart, then back again
Such, is the human condition

Still, what a vision of loveliness
An image, I'll ever save
The picture of perfection, I must confess
And I'll take it to my grave

The Stalker

What will be his plan, today
To catch me in his snare?
Perhaps, display his 'golden tongue'
Then, try and touch my hair?

I feel the presence of his eyes
Everywhere I go
Ever watching, ever piercing
Right down to my soul

I try to act nonchalant
Whenever he is near
But my heart, emits a heavy sound
I pray, he cannot hear

I ponder, why he picked me out
Was it something that I said?
That makes him think, he has a chance
To gain my love, and then my bed

Is this my wage for being nice
This 'crawling of my skin'?
Compassion...my solitary vise
Friendship...my only sin

I pray that he will understand
When I ask him to retreat
Departing from his 'ego trip'
And be not indiscreet

I write this poem, devoid of names
Your character, not to mar
None may ever guess the truth
But, you know who you are

Born Again

As I contemplate my life
(A bittersweet existence)
From enmity and strife
I never kept my distance

I knew, this sort of life
Was pointless and immaterial
But, when love affairs are rife
Who can think of things, ethereal?

So ever deeper, I did fall
Into the bottomless pit, of depravity
Never thinking, my friend, at all
Of the consequence and the gravity

Each and every tasteless act
Of seduction and debauchery
Was pleasant, but in fact
Contentment, never brought to me

I was tired of playing the gigolo
To women of means and breeding
Each night was fun and games, although
The 'writing on the wall' I was reading

It wasn't the fault, of each lovely dame
(Those poor, misguided lasses)
I alone, must assume the blame
For seeing the world, through 'rose-colored glasses'

Of this sordid life, I was so fond
I never commenced, to thinking
Of the waste, and emptiness beyond
Or, to what depths, I was sinking

If I didn't pull out of this malaise
Of self-pity, and depression
I'd be leading this life, for the rest of my days
One of constant regression

This lecherous life, is my bane
Sure to be my undoing
I must assume another vein
For, the present one, I am ruing

I sought to find a woman, you see
Who would fill my life with joy
One to bring out the best in me
To whom, love was not a toy

I'D stop by every lounge and haunt
That I thought, a lovely lady would
My nectared song, I would flaunt
As loud and as often, as I could

I felt, that sooner or later
If the right cards, I did play
A lady, to me, would cater
And come to me, without delay

She's not lead me down, the primrose path
Of hedonistic pleasure
Like every other woman hath
To toy with, at their leisure
I knew that I was charming and witty
I've often been told as much
But wouldn't it be a pity
If somehow, I'd lost my touch

If I can ever leave this perch
Of arrogance and pride
I won't be left, 'standing in the lurch'
And eventually, 'stem the tide'

Alas, a rainbow, may be on the rise
From across the room, a look, she's lending
On me, she has her eyes
Can I read the sign she's sending?

Could it be, my life has value
To one other than myself?
Perhaps, to this charming girl, who
Leaves her pride on the shelf

My friend, she never puts on airs
Arrogance, she does not know
Gloominess—it does not dare
Its dusky face, to show

I feel, that I have been reborn
How completely, I've evolved
No longer lost and forlorn
To avoid apathy, I've resolved

I'm thankful for another chance
To better my present position
This can only serve to enhance
My fortuity, in escaping perdition

*Dark Illusions

Most people are afraid of the darkness
Of the bleak, and forbidding starkness
Though they put up a front,
and try to be brave
Their heart in them, just won't behave
They hear an owl, or some
other night bird
Is this the voice of hell, trying to be heard?
Why are they here...they've
all but forgotten
With knees of jelly...mouths of cotton

l, my friend, am no exception
When it comes to this shadowy deception
I try very hard, to rationalize-
This baseless fear, I can't disguise
When I walk down a murky flight
Or a boulevard, without much light
I always feel, there is someone waiting
To spring a trap, that for
me, they are baiting

I feign all form of demeanor
And my mind is never keener-
Than when I traverse a darkened street
And my paranoia becomes complete
'll contort my face; my lips, I'll purse
No, wait, that could be even worse
If I make a sound, they'll know I'm here
And make manifest, my most ardent fear

I hold my breath, my chest never heaves
And then I go, and step on some leaves

It made such a clamor — Fait accompli
It was then, my adrenalin took off in me
With pulse racing, and heart pounding
Sweat dripping, and head resounding-
My senses, more acute than ever before
Filled with things, that I did abhor

Up my spine, I feel a shiver
When, the first blow, would he deliver?
I was sure a pummeling, would be dealt
Upon me, what sort of
missile, would they pelt?
I tell myself, to get a grip
Nerves of steel — stiff upper lip
All these schemes, sound good, in theory
But not while walking, in
a place that's dreary
Spying a figure coming toward

I entreat my God, "help me, Lord"
Let him pass, without contention
And allay for a time, my apprehension
As he nears, my sinews tense
Not to slacken, from this time, hence
I must be ready, for all provocation
Of courage, I hope there is no privation

Should I nod, or make eye contact?
With lurid thoughts, my mind is wracked
If I look straight ahead, I may not see-
His hands, and what they may do to me
Should I not look, and thus be throttled
And keep my fears, securely bottled

Or should I smile, gratuitously
Thus, throwing him off guard, you see?

As he passes, without event
No more alarm, to my heart, is lent
I offer a sigh, and a silent prayer-
That I won't succumb, to a future snare
As I walk away, from my perceived demise
My panic abates, and my spirits rise
At the next corner, I may be deceived
But as for now, I feel greatly relieved

Feeling smug — my behavior, I'm lauding
Knowing, for now, terror, I'm defrauding
From its fatal grip, on my heart and mind
To peace and serenity, I'm now resigned
My once labored breath, under control
Reaching home safely, is my only goal
Just a few steps, and I'll end this race
Wrapped in my family's loving embrace

What a night I've had; a trying tale to tell
How I barely escaped, the very jaws of hell
Oh, how I long for some pretzels and foam
And those three little words:
'hey, daddy's home"

'High' Fidelity

Most men want to wed, 'the girl next door'
I am no exception
Someone with class and charm, and more
A woman, close to perfection

All these traits, in you, I found
You've answered all my dreams
By the Grace of God, we were bound
You were meant for me, it seems

You've given me joy, and peace of mind
Much more than I could expect
I'm glad, that with you, I was aligned
And I often take time to reflect-

Upon this one, who shares my bed
My fancies, and my plans
And wipes away the tears I shed
With soft and gentle hands

In my heart, you tend to evoke
Every emotion, a man can feel
The fire in me, you forever stoke
When, upon my lips, you affix your seal

Children, too, you've borne, my dear
The fruit of our sacred bond
Yes, you've taken me to a new frontier
Even several steps beyond

To express my love, my cherished mate
I tell you this — now hear it
My soul, you raise to a higher state
Not heaven, perhaps —yet, near it

Foolish Pride

Once, my heart was cold and hard
With no intent to soften
Compassion, was kept at bay
And I was alone, quite often

Upon my shoulder, there was a chip
The biggest one around
I carried it, with the utmost pride
Weighing a ton, if it weighed a pound

I'd flaunt it everywhere
To everyone I'd see
Though, my true nature, it did not reflect
Therein, lies the irony

I have a kind and gentle heart
Though, never showing proof
Keeping my meekness, tucked inside
I was arrogant and aloof

The world was wrong, I was always right
Period — End of story
When speaking of life, I'd wag my head
Each word...derogatory

I cared not, if I made a friend
The problem, I felt, was theirs
Those biting remarks, behind my back
The coldness, and the stares-

All served to fuel my marked distrust
Of all humankind

About my plight, I'd rail and swear
Never having peace of mind

It was a sad, and lonely life
This, I can't deny
But, I made this 'bed of sorrow'
So, in it, I must lie

I truly felt, I had no choice
But, to continue with this sham
Keeping the 'inner man', locked inside
Never showing, who I really am

I owed it to the ones who cared
The ones who really mattered
Family and friends, didn't merit one
Who's life was torn and tattered

They deserve a better men
Than I've been, up 'til now
Their faith in me, warms my heart
I must change for them, somehow

I must form a special bond
And by the spirit, be led
Allowing God to show the way
Then all is possible, it's said

I can be a benevolent man
Not a boor, or offender
With a different persona, everyday
A charlatan — a pretender

I vow to change my point of view
Ever striving toward that end
I want to live in a world, where
Every man will call me, friend

I have progressed, of this I'm sure
Much of my life, I've bettered
I have less bitterness, in my heart
It's now softer, and unfettered

I see these effects, more and more
From every cheerful display-
Of love and concern, for everyone
Someone smiled at me, today

I know, I've got a ways to go
To fulfill my destiny
And though, I'm not there, yet
I'm not where I used to be

Day by day, I'll take up my cross
And walk the narrow aisle
Each good deed, will steel me
'Til, with God, I reconcile

The Altruist

Helping people all I could
I felt, that was my gift
Weaving smiles, and doing good
Giving their day a lift

When a friend would say, "I need a hand"
I'd tell them, "count on me"
I'd never balk —they'd misunderstand
If I offered an apology

So off I'd go, this gallant knight
To be at their 'beck and call'
...answer all their pleas, forthright
No task would be too tall

Running here, running there
And seldom slowing down
With everyone, myself, I'd share
I wore a heavy crown

I was so busy 'giving out'
While never 'giving in'
That I never really thought about
Spreading myself too thin

Every time, I felt that way
I'd intensify the pace
Helping two or three a day
In a constant state of grace

I've been told, I shouldn't be
Saving every life
Put that time and energy

Towards my kids and wife

They say, they're just being kind
While I was so contrary
"How can you be so blind?"
Time and time, we'd parry

My selfless motives, they malign
I have an ulterior plan
Each act performed by design
To deceive my fellow man

These accusations, are not true
Why can't I make them see?
Each helping hand, hitherto
Has been given, generously

I realize, the day may come
When I may lose desire
My senses may go numb
And apathy, quench the fire

Until that day, I'll be a font
Spewing joy and love
Filling all need and want
With a little help, from above

Temptation

I needed you not, to enter my life
But darling, there you were
Happy was l, with my lovely wife
Contented, to be with her

Though I must admit, most nights were cool
And apathy cloaked our bed
Conversing, silence would overrule
And things were left unsaid

Niceties, were seldom exchanged
Each was taken for granted
We were quickly becoming estranged
'l love you," was seldom chanted

I felt the need, to explore
Break free from that 'ball and chain'
I hadn't the desire, theretofore
Now, lewd thoughts, did I entertain

I'd see you dear, many times
Your beauty...often pondered
Of the kind written, in story and rhymes
And I confess, my mind had wandered

You noticed me, too, and I could tell
My attentions, you desired
With heart racing, 'pell-mell'
Old passions, anew, you fired

I told you of my nuptial woes
(Bending a sympathetic ear)
Of how my marriage was in its 'throes'
And about to disappear

You caressed me, dear, and kissed me gently
Sweeter lips, I'd never tasted
You wanted this affair — evidently
My overtures, had not been wasted

The stage was set, the time was right
To be more than casual friends
It was carnality, at its height
And about to pay dividends

We'd share ourselves, most every night
Our passion was exhausting
I felt, not at all contrite
Not caring, what it was costing

By leading this double-life, I knew
My world, It would complicate
But I took the hedonistic view
And kept entering heaven's gate

The nights I had with you-
Were nothing short of magic
Though, I'd scored a major coup
My life was becoming tragic

As our torrid affair, swiftly progressed
I thought I'd be more at ease
Yet, to myself I had confessed
It felt more like profanity and sleaze
My heart told me, I must withdraw
Yet, I languished 'neath your spell
I suppose, of you, I was still in awe
Buying the 'bill of goods,' you had to sell

Still, I knew, for my family's sake
I must quickly regain my senses
Correct this base, and shameful mistake
Go home, and start 'mending fences'

The grass is e'er a brighter green
In someone else's yard
Now, here I stand, with hands unclean
And character, slightly marred

I pray to God, it's not too late
To glean the scattered pieces
Of a bond, that once was great
Despite my many caprices

We met today, on the street
You smiled, and called my name
"Let's stop, and get a bite to eat'
"No, thank you, just the same"

These days, my dear, my head's on straight
Nevermore, to quail and quibble
Where once, I eagerly took the bait
Now, I won't even nibble

Second Chance

A woman of moderate years
Spent much of her life in tears
And those that she shed
At night in her bed...
The silent pain, that nobody hears

The reasons her heart was aching
Were partly of her own making
Alcohol and drugs
(Those dastardly thugs)
Like a thief, her life, was taking

She drank, to forget her sorrow
Her courage, from a bottle, she'd borrow
Lamenting her plight
Giving up the fight
For a bright and sunny tomorrow

In, the foul liquid, she'd pour
'Til her body couldn't take anymore
Instead of calling a truce
All hell broke loose
Her systems, were declaring war

The limit, finally was reached
Her organs, were thoroughly breached
For her to survive
A miracle must arrive
So, her Lord, she humbly beseeched

Praying for Him to save her
She needed a heavenly waiver
From all past transgressions

And marked indiscretions
Now, she needed just one more favor

To have this bitter cup be taken
From His servant - So forsaken
If spared from this death
She could take another breath
And to a bright new day, awaken

If she was given another chance
She would assume a different stance
The change would be striking
And more to His liking
There was much, she could
'bring to the dance'

Though she pondered the
concept of dying
For her children's future, she was vying
They needed her direction
And motherly protection
So, on His mercy, she was relying

He answered her prayers, posthaste
Such devotion, He didn't want to waste
Now, on firm ground, she's treading
Toward salvation, she's heading
His favor, on her, He's placed

The moment she was reprieved
A sigh of relief, was heaved
Though she triumphed, this day
She must now repay
For all the blessings received

Alcohol, she planned to forsake
Never again, to make that mistake
To use it as a crutch-
For escape - inasmuch-
As a vow to God, she can't break

She told me, she hadn't imbibed
Since that day, when she nose-dived
I believe her- I must!
There is no friendship, without trust
Thank God - I think she's arrived

Up from the dregs, she's risen
Escaping her self-imposed prison
Keeping her head from the noose
Of substance abuse
She's made her final decision

To walk in the light - not the shade
Where her lovely radiance, will never fade
A virtual beacon
That will never weaken
But forever be displayed

God, grant her every amenity
And keep her from all obscenity
Your daughter...caress
Her heart, may you bless
'Til she sleeps with you, in serenity

The Final Chapter

This alliance that we have
Has evolved, dear, in stages
And of them, I could write a book
Come, and turn the pages

When we first met, my heart was yours
Of you alone, I'd dream
You were the briskness, in my step
In my eye, the gleam

When e'er you touched me, dear
My curried ego, soared
The world was then, a better place
And in it, I was lord

The next phase, of this love affair
Appeared a bit one-sided
Gone, it seemed, those tender days
When we nestled and confided

Boldly entered number two
A man with looks and brawn
How could I compete with him
This impudent ' walk-on'?

All that glitters, is not gold
It may be glass and smoke
How could I get through to you
Don't fix what isn't broke?

I felt, that I could win you back
If given half the chance
Perhaps you'd turn, and realize
Who brought you to the dance

I would mount one final charge
And wait with 'bated breath'
Though, I felt the answer, I may get
And it scared me, half to death

Then you said, I should not see
Or call you, anymore
Those words were caustic, to my ears
I whimpered, and I swore

I cursed the ground, you walked upon
With black and cloven hoof
Beguiling angel, born in hell
Pernicious and aloof

Diverse emotions, slowly wane
As sanity returns
This latest bridge, is coming down
I watch it, as it burns

The final chapter, of my book
(A haunting elegy)
The end of love, which could have been
That I can now foresee

I dot the I's, and cross the T's
The story finally ends
You'll have to wonder, if my heart
Breaks apart, or mends

When I write the sequel to my book-
You will not be there
Is there life after you?
Read it— if you dare

Doubters Never Dance

When I begin a new adventure
Someone's always there to censure
I'm not adept or smart enough
They remark, in a voice so gruff

In lieu of getting their support
My dreams, they try to thwart
To me, a little credit, give
For at least, taking the initiative

Those callous folk, with narrow mind
Tongue so sharp, and eye so blind
Devoid of faith, and short on vision
Dare attack me with derision

Don't they want me to succeed
Or, on my failure, do they feed?
When I need to be inspired
In a sea of scorn, I am mired

It's not so much, my friends, you see
But the taunting of my family
To find that water, is thicker than blood
Dealt my heart, a mighty thud

The very ones, which I hold dear
Deny and scoff, each new frontier
I feel disillusioned and betrayed
But now, the 'ground rules' have been laid

On help from home, I can't depend
So on my own, I must fend
If I succeed, or if I fail
My fervor, they cannot curtail

I'll continue spawning schemes
Playing hunches...following dreams
When I'm told, It's 'pie-in-the-sky'
I won't relent — oh no, not I

I know, one day, I'll show them all
When I won't fumble, or 'drop the ball'
They'll rue the day, each
'Doubting Thomas'
For not believing - This, I promise

Let them mock me, if they must
They've often jeered, railed and cussed
Despite their wild, derisive chants
When I hear my 'song', I'll
get up and 'dance'

A 'Moving Experience

A man ascending a stairway
One hot summer afternoon
Had trouble maintaining his airway
Getting tired, way too soon

He was wheezing and panting
But vowed, somehow, he'd make it
Halfway up, he began recanting
And decided, he just couldn't fake it

If the stairs worked with
me, and not against
I'd get to the top much faster
Of this fancy, I'm convinced
Then, I could be their master

After finally getting to the top
An hour or so later
He invented a stair, which
would never stop
He called it an escalator

The early riders of this moving stair
(With feet firmly planted)
Welcomed it, with much fanfare
But now-days, it's taken for granted

We ride it up...We ride it down
It's surely, one of man's farces
You can find one, in any large town
To help move our lazy arses

What's the point, anyhow?
They go so very slow
Though, to the gods of ingenuity, we bow
As sluggishly up the stairs, we go

We could reach the top quite rapidly
If we'd only use our gams
Instead, we proceed more vapidly
Like a bunch of hapless lambs

As we near the top, we get more pensive
Concerning the last step, of the flight
About stepping off, we're apprehensive
Those darn things can bite!

When at last, we reach our destination
We feel much relieved, although
Imagine our utter consternation
If someone saw us stub our toe

Let's see now, what did we really save
By taking this undulating machine?
Did we save time, oh, behave!
A bigger waste, I've never seen

Some say, "we saved our legs
Our bodies, we must care for"
I say, nay, use your pegs
Verily, that's what they're there for

In some circles, it's called a boon
For the betterment of mankind
Well, the time may come, very soon
When they'll wake up one day and find-

A blackout, has just hit town
And electricity is in disrepair
Those haughty folk, will say, with a frown
"We have to use the stair"

Indiscretions

I'm a complicated man
With everything to hide
What I lack in wisdom
I make up for in pride

I'm not a 'dream come true'
Though, I fancy that I am
Relying on my innate charm
To perpetuate this sham

You see, there I go again
Flaunting my conceit
I can sometimes be a boor
And often, indiscreet

My life is but a fantasy
At least, an ample part
Concentrated heavily-
On matters of the heart

To certain women, I am drawn
Becoming too attached
My common sense, takes a hit
Morality dispatched

I have eccentric notions
Of my cunning and my worth
To cajole and tease the fairer sex
Is why I'm here on Earth

That is how I act, at least
Though not rational or just
And by many, to be sure

I'm vilified, and cussed
INDISCRETIONS

They feel that I am quite insane
Because of things I do
And when it comes to decency
I haven't got a clue

I can't blame them, all that much
For thinking this of me
Truly, I'm a married man
And shouldn't stray, you see

But I like women, Heaven knows
Perhaps, a bit too much
At times I break the 'golden rule'
Look, but never touch

This shady fact, I must conceal
From family and friend
In the game of life, I don't play fair
And rules, I often bend

Perhaps, someday, I will get burned
While playing with the fire
All sins and vices, heaped atop
My funerary pyre

It's true, I've led a roguish life
I'm a villain and a sot One
day, I'll put it all behind
Then again, maybe not

Aardvark

Many beasts walk this earth
Those with small, or gigantic girth
Some are regal and stately
Receiving their looks, innately
A few...the objects of mirth

Allow me to make a remark
As we quickly prepare to embark
On this virtual jaunt
To the African haunt
Of the curious-looking aardvark

They are truly an aberration
A highly specialized mutation
They've ears like a mule
And eat ants for fuel
Though, that is not their classification

They are really, one of a kind
With huge claws, fore and hind
A leathery skin
That's more than thin
And a nose that's streamlined

Prowling the savanna for termites
On those sultry African nights
With their elongated snout
They search them out
'Til they've sated their appetites

Meek and mild, by breeding
Though, nothing are they conceding
When thoroughly tested

They're seldom bested
Sending their rivals, battered and bleeding

With sharp and massive claws
An opponent's flesh, it draws
But, if they should lose the fray
They'll be carried away
For, in the jungle, there are no laws

Their plight is becoming grave
These docile creatures, we must save
We should preserve this rarity
For all posterity
And keep this gift, which God gave

All avenues, we must exhaust
Lest their species, forever be lost
If they 'fall through the cracks'
Of apathy, it smacks
And it's man, who bears the cost

God's Gift... ?

A pretty face, will turn my head
Ignite my passion, and keep it fed
I'm not a cad
Or, innately bad
Just a man, born and bred

I'm not averse to flirting
What can it be hurting?
I mean no harm
No cause for alarm
Just my ego, I am asserting

The dialogue doesn't matter
Deep talk, or silly chatter
As we converse
My lines, I rehearse
Oh, what barriers, I can shatter

A gentle kiss - perhaps, a touch
It doesn't really matter, much
Wrong or right
I keep it light
My humor, is my crutch

I present a pleasing style
Devoid of pomp or guile
No character molesting
Only light-hearted jesting
Their honor, trying not to defile

If I appear to them, as 'safe'
Their pride, I will not chafe
They admire my wit
My boldness...acquit
Each housewife, debutant or waif

Though, at times, when talk was lewd
And carnal words from my lips, exude
Not wanting to slant her
Her penchant for banter
Will determine the magnitude

If it seems, I have no shame
My testosterone is to blame
Off I go - undaunted
Vanity, to be flaunted
Flutter hearts - It's in the game

I know there will come a time
When I won't be in my prime
As I near my completion
Of hormonal secretion
...To the ridiculous, from the sublime

When the heat deserts my blood
And I'm left, a romantic dud
I'll often recall
With no trouble, at all
When I was quite the amorous stud

An Eventful Year

When e'er I peruse my reverie
You always seem to be there
Though I try to disguise it, so cleverly
I can't veil the fact...I still care

Dear, I recall the day we met
And first laid eyes, on each other
You were flirting, and beset
By everyone, and his brother

It wasn't hard to understand
How this could come about
You were so charming...thus, in demand
With your coy smile, and cute little pout

Though, it made me ill at ease
To see them leer and drool
I saw, in you, possibilities
Certain, that your heart, I could school

'Twas the vernal equinox
And there was much to discover
Passion kisses, and moonlight walks
Then, I took you as my lover

Love and springtime, coexist
Or so the poets aver
Our love did bloom, in the April mist
We were quite the handsome pair

Our love was of the rarest kind
It transcended the bounds of perfection
A love of both, heart and mind
And they'd move, at our direction

When e'er we heard the robin's trill
We felt, too, that we could fly
What a rush...I can feel it, still
Us, apart, nothing could pry

Flowers, too, we did gather
Crocus and daffodils
Their scents intoxicated us, rather
Our senses, they did fill

In early June, we took a hiatus
To that lonely tropic isle
Our passion was great...
nothing could sate us
So there we stayed, for awhile

When it came time, we hated to depart
Leaving this 'Eden in the round'
And here's a remembrance
straight from the heart
The quintessence of a paradise found

Those hot summer days, which
caused us to swelter
Nights, cooled by an ocean breeze
This heart in me, ever will shelter
Fond memories, such as these

Autumn came...we were still together
But I noticed in you, a change
It seemed the bloom, was off the heather
Priorities, you'd rearranged

At times, you'd seem so cold and distant
Was this just a phase?
To my advances, you were more resistant
I could see boredom, in your gaze

Had I misjudged so terribly
Could I have been so utterly wrong?
My heart is weeping, unbearably
But for appearances, I must be strong

This affair, was seemingly my bane
With this woman, in my charge
A romance, which was once a hydro-plane
Has become a lumbering barge

I clung to her steadfastly
As one holds onto a vision
I felt that she was judging me
And I dreaded the decision

Had I done something, that offended her
Or was it her propensity
Was this one, a pretender?
It really didn't make sense to me

Had my affections, so devotional
Been entirely for naught?
Presently, I'm getting very emotional
With sorrow, I am fraught

As the winter wind, with its icy fingers
Chill me to the bone
This heart, in me, where she lingers
Feels so terribly alone

An Eventful Year

Now the trees are bare; the birds are gone
I'm feeling so forlorn
I wake, to find a cold, gray dawn
She left our home, this morn

My despair is great, and still it grows
Though, I will not try to find her
This chapter in my life, is at a close
But I leave this, as a reminder

If it seems too good to be true, I've heard
That's a valid indication
That from the sublime, to the absurd
Is your final destination

As the tears within my heart, abate
And anxieties fade away
May her leaving, in my life, create
Healing — without delay

A Gerbil's Life

There are many critters, you can have as a pet
An iguana, cockatoo or serval
But the best one I've found, yet
Is a roly-poly gerbil

A gerbil is an animal from Africa or Asia
It's kind of hairy and fat
You can watch it for hours, and it will amaze ya
It's like a furry little rat

They're fuzzy and fat —the real deal
With a tail that's elongated
For eating their daily meal
They have teeth that are serrated

A gerbil is a herbivore
Eating leaves and seeds
I must say, I've never been here before
Watching a gerbil, as it feeds

As they feed, their little nose twitches
Like they are smelling, before they partake
Watching them eat, just keeps me in stitches
Seeing the cute little faces they make

I watch them, too, in their little cages
Running on a wheel, to nowhere
How far they run, no one knows
After a while, I just say, "whoa, there"

Ode To A Stuffed Bear

There are many stuffed bears, of various sizes
Some are fat and cuddly, some are svelte
But the one that puts the gleam, in most kids' eyes is
The one named after Teddy Roosevelt

The Teddy Bear, is the yardstick
By which other bears are measured
He is the one, most would pick
To be loved, cherished, and treasured

Teddy is not the only bear
That makes kids dribble and drool
There are others, so let's be fair
Some are equally as cool

The musical bear, is just a bear
With tunes added, for effect
Often, something else goes in there
A voice, with a strange dialect

You've got bears that play, talk, and crawl
And you've got, just plain Teddy
Just when you think, we've covered them all
I've just thought of more — are you ready?

I can't forget the hunters, out there
The dauntless, big game shooter
Next to a cuddly Teddy Bear
He'll say that, his is cuter

To see these noble giants, used this way
Me, it does abhor
When people put them on display
To enhance their rec-room floor

I hope you don't think, I'm 'off-the-wall'
Or, I've put something in my stogy
But, the most lovable stuffed bear of all
Is your friend, and mine — Yogi!

Prim and Proper

I recall, when I was young
Brandishing my 'silver tongue'
To woo a girl, with style and form
I excelled at that - it was the norm

We'd view a girl, with regard
And play the troubadour or bard
E'er forsake the teenybopper
Everything was prim and proper

To hold her hand, and watch her eyes
See her smiles, hear her sighs
Such were the passions of my youth
Mixed with wisdom, and with truth

In olden days, it was an art
To keep the horse, before the cart
Today, apathy is the curse
That turns this cliché, in reverse

When courting a girl, in modern times
Her heart's not won, with song and rhymes
Likewise, pomp and circumstance
Have given way to 'song and dance'

To the girls, I must be blunt
You share the blame, for this affront
Without a word of reprimand
You take each slight, and let it stand

Girls, nowadays, don't seem to care
If men demean, and overbear
They play the hand, that they are dealt
Though, on their pride, it leaves a welt

In my day, thoughts were clean
We'd treat each girl, like a queen
A goddess fair, and here's the topper
Everything was prim and proper

Poem To A Grecian Lady

If ever I made you, ill at ease
Forgive me, dear, I beg you, please
If I said something, that wounded you
And you hurt, then I hurt, too

Your friendship, has a special place
In my heart, where I save a space
Near the people, who I want to remember
Until life becomes a dying ember

When e'er I see your smiling face-
My heart transcends to a higher place
Mount Olympus, high and mighty
Where I see the goddess, Aphrodite

All bedecked in golden hue
Statuesque, and charming, too
Her face and form, are classic Greek
It's you, my dear, of whom I speak

As Argonauts, of ancient Greece
Who sought, and found, the 'golden fleece'
I have found, in you, the greatest prize
About which, men fantasize

As we return, where mortals tread
Oft recall the words, I've said
And keep me in your reverie
That's where I long, to ever be

My Wife-My Bride

My wife is more, than just my bride
Who cleans, and cooks my dinner
She can also, stroke my pride
And tell me, I'm a winner

Each day, a home for me, she makes
At night, she shares my pillow
Our love oft bends, but never breaks
Like a lithy, swaying willow

When I come home, late at night
And she asks me, how I'm feeling
I have to smile at her in spite
Of a tough day, from which I'm reeling

She always knows, just what to say
To soothe the savage beast in me
On my mind, she knows how to play
Stirring emotions, I thought had ceased in me

She has the magic touch, you see
Of one who truly loves
And my heart takes flight — Verily
On the wings, of snow-white doves

Confessions of A Rogue

Once again, I rue the day
My flippant tongue, got in the way
With talk so glib..
(A loose ad-lib)
Kind hearts, I do betray

This dreadful curse,
I cannot lose
My arrogant heart, it imbues
I'm no sooner fraught
With a covetous thought
Than, another one debuts

I'm not a lecherous man
With a cruel and sadistic plan
Just a hopeless romantic
Whose ego's gigantic
And a character, not 'spic and span'

I've a slightly checkered past
As a feminine enthusiast ..
Tarnished my name
But, just the same
To this life, I've remained steadfast

With the women, I enjoy a flirt
Both discreetly and overt
Pretty or plain
I don't abstain
Anything in a skirt

I mean them no disrespect
Nor, to insult their intellect

But this knack, I possess
Vanity to excess
For too long, has gone unchecked

I've lost face with colleagues and friends
To the depths, my honor descends
I must come to grips
With these proprietary slips
Repent, and make amends

I'm sure I can 'stem the tide'
And discard this foolish pride
My only task...
Shed this trifling mask
Don sobriety, and 'let it ride'

When my style, I rearrange
And the good for the bad, exchange
Alter my scheme
Show the ladies, more esteem
Then my friends, no more, I'll estrange

I'm sure it will take some time
But their opinion of me, will climb
Nevermore the assaulter
Just a constant exalter
From the ridiculous, to the sublime

There's a moral to my tale
For each and every male
With each wanton remark
Resentment, it may spark
In your coffin...another nail

So, if you're always feeling spurned
By the people, that you've burned
Don't whimper and whine
Curse and malign
.A lesson to be learned

If on guile, you do rely
The day may be drawing nigh
When you'll begin a skid
And find, as I did
Talk is cheap, but the price is high

Obsession

Dear, you captivate my mind
My will, you mold like clay
To the servile life, I have resigned
It's every whim, I will obey

Your classic face and form, my pet
Send my senses reeling
You're a woman of flesh and bone, and yet
You lift me to the ceiling

And I sha'nt come down, lest you unloose
My heart — but know the gravity
Around its core, you'll tighten a noose
And rend it from its cavity

If you should set me free, my sweet
This man would not be viable
If I am turned into the street
I swear, my dear, I'm liable-

To end this wretched life of mine
Dispatch it with great haste
If, my dear, I can't be thine
Then, to this man, I will lay waste

Expectations

I was once, an angry man
Never hearing love's refrain
Devoid of a comprehensive plan
I was arrogant, self-centered and vain

I was master of my world
Though, a sphere of anguish and grief
If around me, rancor and bitterness curled
My reign would be, but brief

I felt, I'd never find the one
Who would make this man complete
It seemed, the end had just begun
My resolve was in retreat

Then, into my life, this woman came
And stirred up passion's fire
Pleasing her, soon became
My first, and only desire

I'd buy her candy, or a pretty rose
Just like a natural man
Writing words, in rhyme and prose
To this goddess, wrapped in saran'

I longed to touch her golden hair
Her dainty hands, caress
Yet, all I seemed to do was stare
Upon this image of loveliness

So, on a pedestal, I have placed her
This vision, from a poet's dream

Within my heart, I have encased her
Where peace and love, do teem

My senses, have been overpowered
And heightened, to a fever pitch
Expectation now, where
doubt once cowered
A highly fortuitous switch

I truly believe, she feels the same
I see it in her smile
To her, love is not a game
One only plays, for a while

Forever and a day
Our hearts will e'er be tethered
From each other, we'll never stray
With fidelity, our 'nest' will be feathered

This way, I'm sure, it was meant to be
Two hearts ever beating as one
I could say, with the utmost certainty
There was nothing left undone

Save, perhaps, to join our hands
In sacred, wedded bliss
Exchange our matrimonial bands
And seal it with a kiss

The foundation now was laid
The odds have been defied
That I would find this lovely maid
And take her for my bride

Now, I had seen her every day
Since I commenced my wooing
Not once, did she betray
Our clandestine rendezvousing

This is why, I felt it odd
When she failed to keep appearing
Had her feelings for me, been a façade
Was I too attentive...to domineering?

As I pondered, these many queries
That seared my heart and brain
Alas, I had no plausible theories
My reflections, had been in vain

With every failed undertaking
Each dead-end, that I met
A bit more of my heart was breaking
With anxiety, I was beset

At last, I had a revelation
And I inquired of her parents
Hoping to end this worry and frustration
And to learn the cause of her aberrance

They thought, in me, she had confided
The truth about her illness
It was then, uncertainty and panic collided
With a marked and deafening shrillness

"How is she - can I see her, now?"
These words, I kept repeating
I must be near her, somehow
God, tell me - Is this
malady, she defeating?

Expectations

Their chilling words, struck a chord
And cut just like a knife
She made her peace, with her Lord
Then, offered up her life

It's said, you go to a better place
A realm, where you can't be freer
She's there, this one with an angel's face
And someday, I hope to see her

For now, I'll live with memories
For, they are all I've got
And a heartache, I can't appease
For now, this is my lot

Dear, I'm longing for the day
When death will take me, too
It's mournful cry, I will obey
Then, I'll spend eternity with you

Science/Fiction

There are some, who pose the theory
Life began in a pond, dark and dreary
A single cell...less than small
Acknowledged the fate, it could not forestall

This simple form, that did exist
Began the change, say evolutionists
It then developed complexity
And thus, became you and me

That's the claim, these men put down
And soon became, the talk of the town
What a boon to science, these pundits made
But to me, it doesn't make the grade

I need not question, or analyze
Having only to view, earth and skies
To know, there is no reason or rhyme
Why life should emerge, from out the slime

No twist of fate, as they advance
No cataclysmic happenstance
Could forge the wonders, that I see
The grass —A deer — The birds — A tree

The vibrant hues, upon the land
Could only be wrought, by an artist's hand
Beauty and charm, where e're you look
The quiet sea — The babbling brook

The scented rose, the four-leaf clover
I see the hand of God, all over
God, who made the universe
Then gave it to us, for better or worse

I grieve the poor, misguided mind
Who looks for answers, where there are none to find
Time would be much better spent
Reading the Dual Testament

Amber Lynn

Sweet as clover, as it grows
Soft and feminine
Like a virtual budding rose
And the fragrant flower within
Warm as paraffin, as it glows
Amber Lynn — Lovely Amber Lynn

Heart as pure as driven snow
Too, her creamy skin
From her lips, honeyed words do flow
As the strains, of a violin
Sugar and spice — How apropos
Amber Lynn — Beautiful Amber Lynn

Flaxen hair, God did bestow
On this child, with the pleasing grin
Straight on top, curling below
Subject to discipline
Turning the head, of an impetuous beau
Amber Lynn — Charming Amber Lynn

A Wasted Life

When I was a young man
So deep in my prime
I didn't have a plan
There was nothing but time

I'd steal the heart, of many a maiden
Plying them with wine and flowers
Never feeling the least bit remorse-laden
I'd tease them for hours and hours

Pleasing their fancies, and
filling their heads
With tales of "daring-do"
Compromise their values,
and warm their beds
And then, I quickly withdrew

I felt, this life, would last forever
Ever playing the rascal and rogue
Thinking I was so very clever
To me, vulgarity was in vogue

As I kissed their powdered
cheeks and noses
And smelled their perfumed hair
I never stopped, to 'smell the roses'
Though, their scent was in the air

Not that I was looking, you see
I was having too much fun
Parties and such...l was too free
To look for the 'smoking gun'

As days flew by, and turned to years
It seemed, the bloom had faded
I spent more time, drying tears
And I seemed a bit more jaded

Now, all the girls, that I once knew
Throughout that golden age
Over time, somehow, withdrew
Less inclined, to me, engage

We'd speak of matters, trifling
And never of the sublime
The loneliness now, is stifling
Am I a victim of time?

It used to be so easy for me
Looseness, I'd never omit
Now, my friend, it's plain to see
To chivalry, I must commit

Oh, I have a million memories
Of triumphs and near misses
And vestiges, now on the breeze
Of walks and moonlight kisses

I recall, clandestine trysts
With many a lovely lass
But, like a pair of antagonists
We'd always reach an impasse

I'd never made a lasting friend
A partner, a confidant or consort
Mixed messaged, did I send
A portent to abort

Never taking the time to find
My princess, in a crystal slipper
I'd forever seek the other kind
A trollopy day-tripper

As I sit and reminisce
Of a paradise, now lost
I muse, "What manner of man is this"
Choosing pleasure, at any cost

My friend, now as the light grows wane
Shortly to be extinguished
This breath in me, I cannot maintain
Soon, it will be relinquished

So hear me well, my bawdy friend
I leave this as a testament
On charm and wit, do not depend
But, on quality time, well spent

In The Name of Love

I viewed the eyes of love, today
What a feeling of exhilaration
Imbuing me in a special way
(An agreeable infiltration)

The eyes of love, are warm and caring
Not at all, haughty or vain
In their midst, compassion is flaring
Erupting, again and again

I kissed the hand of love, today
As a salutary gesture
That she found my manner sincere, I pray
And, that I genuinely had impressed her

Bowing before her, sounds an alarm
And I'm brought to a state of rapture
I drink in her abundant beauty and charm
As much as my heart can capture

I beheld the countenance of love, today
..decidedly angelic in bearing
Replete, with an ambrosial bouquet
In which, all of my senses are sharing

The embodiment of all, good on earth
This, to the world, I proclaim
Then, everyone will know her worth
For, love, truly is her name

A Promising Career

I had it all, I must confess
The world upon a string
I dreamed of even more success
And the pleasures it would bring

An athlete of the first degree
In high school, and beyond
I had smarts, talent and looks, you see
I was blue-eyed and blonde

I was destined for a great career
In whatever sport I'd choose
It was the wish, of every peer
To walk within my shoes

Then one day, I felt a pain
My leg becoming numb
That eerie feeling, would not wane
But to its threat, I would not succumb

Fatigue must be the cause
Of my weakened state
No inherent flaws
Would keep me from my fate

As time went by, more signs were there
That something wasn't right
This malady did impair
My agility and my sight

It deprives me of each simple chore
Like daily walks, and reading

Doctors say, they can't do more
To abate or 'stop the bleeding'

My very life, is now on hold
I feel helpless, and alone
The fire in me, is growing cold
Toward depression, I am prone

I once enjoyed being alive
(The alternative was much worse)
Now, I've simply lost my drive
And living is a curse

Even though my time's run out
Or perhaps, because of it
I recall with pride, each rousing shout
I thought they'd never quit

Looking back, upon the years
When I was in my prime
I can smile through my tears
Having my 'moment in time'

I miss the whole athletic fare
Each and every tussle
But now I'm in this cold, steel chair
Barely able to move a muscle

I pray each day, for life to end
Endure — I can't much longer
My Blessed Lord, your angels, send
Oh, if I were stronger!

I know, I shouldn't feel this way
(The frustration and the dread)
It's now come down to the final play
And I'm hanging by a thread

But, I'm now willing, to meet my fate
My soul...my humble token
And with my God, I will create
A ring of love, unbroken

The Lonely Deer Hunter

Up before dawn, no time to loiter
Must step outside, and reconnoiter
Checking the air...scanning the ground
For signs that a deer, may be around

Hoping it snowed, the night before
Making it easier, to follow his spore
You go back inside, for the
rest of your gear
Thinking all the while, "just
bring on the deer"

A last look around, before you head out
Must think positive; no room for doubt
One thought in mind, as you exit the door
"I'll come back empty-handed, no more"

You find a trail, which looks to be fresh
This is your day, to exact
your 'pound of flesh'
You feel it in your bones —
Man, what a thrill
Or maybe, it's just the cold
November chill

It matters not, to the hardy deer slayer
If you want to score, you must be a player
So on you go, through the
briar and the bramble
Knowing all the while, that
it's really a gamble

You stop for a time, and survey the land
Looking for a tree, for to
put up your stand

You find one, that's strategically placed
Scampering up it, with
the greatest of haste

You hurry, to secure your perch
.Don't want to be left,
'standing in the lurch'
Sitting there for hours, waiting for a buck
A plum, from the tree of life,
you're hoping to pluck

At times like these, a man gets reflective
Putting his life into perspective
You muse of your wife, in your reverie
The children, too, each and every

The joys of life, you're now reminiscing
Your family's cheeks, you
long to be kissing
You'll soon be home, to tuck them in bed
There are hugs to be given,
stories to be read

Friends, you have, and blessings, galore
Who could ever ask for more?
With tis so strong, they will not sever
Good friends are like diamonds
— They are forever

Suddenly, something breaks
your concentration
It could be the moment of jubilation
A twig snaps...down below, a rustle
Raising your arms, you
bring up the "muscle'

Then you see him, out a clearing
You hold your breath, as he is nearing
The anxiety you're feeling,
   you can't rescind
All the while, hoping you're upwind

You notice at once, his meagerness of rack
When you get home, you
   may take some flak
First things first; with this
   foe, you must cope
Firming your grip, you get
   him in your scope

There you sit, up in the booth
About to face, the moment of truth
Just for a second, your breath, you hold
Your lifelong dream, about to unfold

You steady yourself — You pull the trigger
Adrenaline flows, with such vim and vigor
That from your perch, you nearly tumble
Catching yourself...down you rumble

You feel, you've dealt him a mighty blow
Off through the woods,
   you're bound to go
When reason stops, and adrenaline rushes
And from his side, life-blood gushes-

He may run a hundred yards, or more
You never know what's in store
Your heart beats faster, as his gives out
His flesh was weak, but his spirit was stout

You find him, in his final throes
This chapter of his life, you soon will close
With knife in hand, you quickly lay waste
Dispatching him, with the utmost haste

The Lonely Deer Hunter

As you dress him out...this forest denizen
Your taste buds tingle...ahh, venison
Chops and loins, and even some steak
And, oh what a trophy, his head will make

As you drag him back, to your humble camp
Tired and dirty, and a little damp-
You salute him, in your special way
For waging a good fight, this winter's day

What a beautiful animal, you think to yourself
"It's too bad, he has to be food on my she f"
Though, if not for me, he'd die of privation
Or some equally heinous situation

As you sit, and partake of your prize-
You think to yourself, how quickly time flies
You comment, to your significant other
"Next year, perhaps, I'll bring home his brother"

Words of Love

My dear, I feel such a fool
Not knowing what to say to you
I'm not this way, as a rule
But each day seems déjà vu

If I uttered something clever or cute
I'd not be apprehensive
Our seared friendship, would then bear fruit
And my joy, would be extensive

It would tell of how I yearn
My dreams and my desires
Of how this passion in me, does burn
With the heat of a thousand fires

I wish I had some fancy word
To whisk you off your feet
One of which, you've never heard
That sounds so very sweet

I rue, I do not have one, dear
Alas, I'm not a poet
Though if I were, this much is clear
Upon you, I would bestow it

My Friend, Jack

I have a friend, his name is Jack
He lives near me, in a one-room shack
Though his abode, was nearly unfurnished
I always helped him, keep it burnished

With spit and polish, and elbow grease
We'd clean every nook, crevice and crease
Jack didn't do much in the way of work
But I'd really not mind, if
a task he would shirk

For, I enjoyed his company so much
It mattered not, if a broom, he'd not touch
When the job was done,
we'd have some grub
A hearty meal, he'd not snub

He never held a job, or had
worldly possessions
But for his shabby appearance,
he made no confessions
Jack was a rover, a real free spirit
Though the world be cruel,
he never would fear it

He'd never let anything get him down
Making me laugh, when playing the clown
I'd laugh so hard, my sides would split
Jack was a caution, and on top of it-

A loyal friend, of the rarest breed
He gives of himself, upon which I feed
From deep inside, compassion emanates

The love in his heart, he
freely disseminates

Some people look down on
him, and they say:
"Who is this bastardly one, anyway/'
They mocked his lineage,
and even his color
Somewhat like ebony, but a little bit duller

It's true, Jack's parents, never were married
But he has a name, and
with pride, It's carried
He's noble and stately, despite all derision
Though with bad luck, he's
had many a collision

His parents split up; since
then, he's wandered
If he would find a home,
I'm sure he's pondered
To our door one day, this transient came
Since then, my life's not been the same

He was dirty and rather louse-ridden
Jack was a mess, and I'm not kiddin'
He got a bath, and a healthy repast
Of which he partook, as if his last

When he ate, we thought he'd go
He started to — but, no
He turned, and to our surprise
Stood there, with dreary eyes

He looked at us, and we could tell
He wanted not, to say farewell
We called, "hey, come on back"
Since then, It's been me and Jack

Some men came, the other day
Intent on taking poor Jack away
They said he was a vagrant
And other charges, more flagrant

They wanted to put him in the pen
Things looked bad, and then
A judge, with mercy as his guide
Said of the charges, "let them slide"

Jack expressed his very own plaudit
Ambiguous, if only the judge caught it
He could leave, under our supervision
An amicable, and fortunate decision

There was much laughter and tears
But less playing; he was up in years
The spirit was willing, but the flesh, weak
We knew, his outlook was bleak

This could not be the end, surely
He was always so robust and burly
Jack could out hunt and run any man
To me, he was life — even bigger than

Passing away in his slumber
Pain, no more, would him, encumber
...Peaceful, lying there, because
We crossed each of his four little paws

The Winds of Fate

The empty space within my bed
Torments me, so - I feel half-dead
Now, every dawn
I find you gone
Each day, is filled with dread

Since you've been taken from my side
There's no place for me to hide
Save, in my mind
Where I find
Reality and faith collide

I've not before, been on my own
But now, the winds of fate, have blown
The gale is strong
As I'm pushed along
Can I reap, what life has sown?

With two small kids, and little skill
I have to make a living, still
One thing is clear
I must persevere
For, my future's all uphill

Jobs are few and far between
Dead-end, too, from all I've seen
But, I swear
I'll take what's there
Now that times are lean

Life is now, touch and go
My darling one, I miss you, so
I see your face

Most every place
I just want you to know

You were my rock...my driving force
And, for your sake, I'll stay-the-course
I'll pray aloud
To make you proud
Such conduct, you'd endorse

For our kids, I will be strong
Against what e'er may come along
I'll keep hope confined
Here, in my mind
And on my lips, a song

A Time In The Life...

Softly we fall, throughout the region
My brothers and I - for we are legion
Covering the land, with a frosty coating
The winter season, we are promoting

As we descend, we take our chances
While constantly giving, peripheral glances
The life of a flake, is tenuous, at best
Wherever we land, we're put to the test

The unlucky ones, land on a road
Unceremoniously, squashed like a toad
Others, a sidewalk's face, they may brush
Where, too, they're turned to slush

The fortunate ones, fall on greenery
Take a breath, and enjoy the scenery
It's a fact, that if you land on clover
There's less chance, of being run over

If you land on a hill, meadow or lawn
Much of your apprehension is gone
Gracing these spots, can add to one's life
Though, even here, dangers are rife

Children playing, skiing or sledding
It's to a martyr's death, we're heading
Yielding ourselves, for human enjoyment
All are subject, to a brief employment

We may be rolled into a neat little ball
(If part of an appreciable fall)
Becoming a victim, of manual compression
Then hurled at a rival, whose face we may freshen

If one escapes every abnormal occurrence
A natural foe, may sap our endurance
As the storied vampire, when morning is nigh
A ray of sunlight, and we may die

Some are glad, to see us leave
Though, while some gloat, others grieve
Saddened to see winter's finale
But when nature calls, one mustn't dally

In due season, we'll be returning
To our earthly abode - sojourning
Some think us needless and vexing, although
For imparting beauty, there's nothing like snow

Unrequiited Emotions

I recall, that many years ago
When I was so much younger
A women flashed her eyes at me
And aroused a latent hunger

A smile, a word, a gentle touch
She gave me these and more
Passion filled my heart and mind
My discretion, on the floor

I felt she was seducing me
From her flaunts, I did not hide
Never caring that I could lose-
My dignity and my pride

My heart and mind were imbued
With thoughts of conquest, but alas-
She didn't want me in that way
So, it never came to pass

When she moved on, there was another
And more came after her
But all took flight, eventually
Their wrath, I did incur

How could they abandon me
After everything I gave?
Their slightest wish, was my command
I'd be their eager slave

Perhaps what people say is true
My manner, is my bane

With every over-attentive act
Emotions, do I strain

I carry friendships to extremes
With feelings, unrequited
So when they tire, and fall away-
I'm left chagrined and slighted

Pride and over-zealousnessWhen
Has closed so many doors
Though, for each one, I shed a tear
The one I rue the most, is yours

I'm sure you thought, I wanted more
Than friendly conversation
And I put you, dear, at the very least
In an awkward situation

Do you tell me of your fears
Or keep them under wraps?
Could this problem be resolved
Or would it all collapse?

These things, I've also pondered
Would it ever be the same
As when our accord was brand new
Innocent and tame?

Now, the sparkle in your eye is gone
Where once it shone so bright
It's luster made my ego feel
Higher than a kite

Once we were not afraid to talk
To smile and to touch
Now we are like strangers
I miss those days, so much

Dear, I know what I must do
To have those days return
Having you feel at ease with me
Is my sole concern

I will never be content
'til I repair this rend
And you can say, with joyful heart
"Let's talk awhile, my friend

A Frog's Frog

In the real world, frogs are seldom seen
They're slippery and wet, and kind of green
Most of them, don't become celebrities
From the Marianas, to the Hebrides

There is one exception, to this amphibian rule
The 'missing link', from the Froggy gene pool
He's greener than some, bigger than most
And his own t.v. show, of which he can boast

This frog, you see, is quite loquacious
Helped by the fact, that his mouth is so spacious H
He can talk for hours, and never get tired
If you didn't know better, you'd think he was 'wired'

The world on a string, had this noble fly-catcher
He was humble and meek, never playing the lecher
Forever being hounded, by a lascivious prig
This 'soiled dove', you see, was a literal pig

In lieu of men like Einstein and Fermi
She chose to stalk, her poor little Kermie
He would try to crawl, run or hop
But it was hard to avoid, her devastating 'pork chop'

This hero of ours, had many chums
Some amiable, some were bums
Of grouchy ones, there were quite a few
While gentle ones—one or two

Some were quite docile, like Fozzy Bear
He sang tunes that were just 'fair' musical fare
He was verbose and narcissistic 'to boot'
And he looked real funky, in his mohair suit

They did many shows, but their 'run' was finite
Now, the whole cast must take flight
They'll do movies, and an occasional 'guest shot'
And appear in publications like, 'who's hot, and who's not'

As for Piggy and Kermit's, one-sided affair
They may go off, and live like hermits, somewhere
Together, like Gretel and Hansel
Sorry Kermie, can you say, 'cancel'?

Girl In A Glass Slipper

Drawn to you, I became
As a moth, to a flame
My chest would swell
My head as well
At the mention of your name

I was truly filled with awe
Detecting, not a single flaw
You had beauty, charm and grace
A Cinderella, wrapped in lace
The sweetest girl, I ever saw

In my heart, you were a guest
And I was very soon obsessed
Perhaps, a demon in disguise
Yet, an angel in my eyes
Fair-skinned and golden-tressed

Your lovely face, curtailed my sleep
I'd count your charms, in lieu of sheep
My intent, I would make known
The seeds of love were sewn
I vowed, your love, I'd keep

But friends told me, I must be sure
For a broken heart, there was no cure
I had no guarantee
Was she the one for me
Or merely, the belle du jour?

They could be right, I must confess
My passion was strong, nevertheless
I should take it slow
Status quo
Handle it with finesse

On eagle's wings, would I be borne
Or subject to a life of scorn?
If we lived as one
Would there be sun
Or storm clouds, every morn?

This union, which I planned with you
Would you declare, you want it, too?
If I had a crystal ball, to see
Would it be victory
Or be my 'Waterloo'?

I was forced to make a lover's choice
Air my thoughts, or hold my voice
I had to bring it to a close
So, the former, is the one I chose
Now each day, I rejoice

You told me, that you felt the same
Share my bed, and my name
With mutual trust
And a little lust
You'd keep my heart aflame

A child or two, or three, or four
A life of pleasure, and rapport
All the things
That marriage brings
We'd ponder and explore

It's now been twenty years, or so
We've had our tiffs - don't you know
But you're still my pet
My Juliet
And l, your Romeo

A Close Encounter

There was a girl, I once knew
Large round eyes, with a brownish hue
Tawny skin, and jet-black hair
Surely, not your normal fare

A lively step, a clever wit
That sometimes, threw me off, a bit
With humor, rather off-the-wall
Her sober side, I still recall

From the droll, to sublime
On the ladder, she would climb
We would laugh, then shed a tear
Memories, that I hold dear

Those lengthy drives, the heart-to-hearts
Our love, at times, was off-the-charts
What we had, was sure to last
Tightly bound, and holding fast

Now and then, we'd have a spat
Concerning, either this or that
Nothing much to fret about
Just a lover's tiff, no doubt

Though life was mostly fun and game
At times, the cynic, she became
She would always speak her mind
Caring not, if cruel or kind

The girl was never long on tact
She's hit a nerve, and I'd react
Little barbs, here and there
But then we'd hug, and clear the air

But I could clearly see a trend
More and more, we would contend
We would give and take, and such
Though, I was giving way too much

I think she sensed, and I did, too
This run we had, was nearly through
Many reasons, I could name
But in the end, no one's to blame

No resentment or remorse
That we couldn't stay-the-course
A brief affair, and nothing more
Now it's time to close the door

We were close, for three long years
Alternating, smiles and tears
Our friendship, though not Heaven-sent
Was on the whole, time well spent

Star-Crossed

Idle talk, is how it began
She'd captivate this mortal man
From those sensual conversations
To 'come hither' invitations
I felt she had a plan

From the start, it was fun and game
And the realization, never came
That, if I formed this alliance
Of mutual compliance I could not redact
My life, would not be the same

Though it began with reciprocity
To my life, it became hypocrisy
I knew it not right
Yet, I didn't put up a fight
This juggernaut had too much velocity

Of my senses, I had taken leave
And my heart was on my sleeve
Myself, she enjoyed
With my heart, she had not toyed
At least, that's what I did believe

I continued playing the clown
And it was evident, to everyone in town-
That my integrity would cheapen-
If this plot, did deepen
For, as a harlot, she was renown

She wanted me as a paramour
This woman, a torch, I did carry for
Thinking its flame, everlasting-

My fate, I was casting-
To the wind — But I didn't care anymore

So, off I went, with the Devil's daughter
Like a lamb, to the proverbial slaughter
My mind was imbued-
With thoughts of things lewd
My nerves were becoming tauter

The fire in me, was all-consuming
She felt it too, I was assuming
Very soon, this wench-
Would be mine to clench
For this moment, me, she was grooming

She led me on, with words and more
The seductive clothes, that she wore
How could any man resist
A wanton display, such as this
The gauntlet, was on the floor

If I picked it up, there was no reprieve
From this tangled web, I
was about to weave
This lecherous act
And my dignity,
I'd never retrieve

I continued this alliance, I didn't
Thinking myself, so very clever
Never sensing I could be caught
With fear and doubt, I was not fraught
I wanted this coalition — However

94

When we were alone, and all was set
And I was about to take, my Juliet
Delay, to my mind, came creeping
Into my brain, it was seeping
I wanted to touch her — And yet

My very soul, fear arose in
For this debauchery, why was I chosen?
With heart all abustle
I couldn't move a muscle
My hands, were as frozen

To my mind, I tried to justify
The lack of temerity, I couldn't deny
Our stars were crossed
But all was not lost
Tomorrow — Another try

I knew not, what was to blame
But our tomorrow, never came
She changed her demeanor
This way, I'd never seen her
Her heart was no longer aflame

As for the cause of my fate
I never did ask her, straight
Taking what she gave me
Thinking, something would save me
The situation, I didn't want to exacerbate

Star-Crossed

Years after the fact, I postulate
Why, my ego, she did perforate
Her immediate gratification
Was not met, on that occasion
Her desires, I did not sate

Even though, my heart was bruised
Because of my passion, being refused
What grieves the worst...
I can't be reimbursed-
For the pain, of being used

Though, this man, she did forsake
My friend, make no mistake
In this willful treachery-
And unabashed lechery-
Thank God, I did not partake

I was once, a star-crossed lover
But in the end, I did discover
A liaison, though nice
Is not worth the price
When around you, guilt and remorse do hover

Musings of A Clown

The snow is deep, the night is chilly
My mind does wander, willy-nilly
All cares subside, and worries flee
As I indulge my reverie

Since I'm not priggish or refined
Toward the light side, I'm inclined
Something absurd and off-the-wall
A cerebral free-for-all

I enjoy a riddle, rhyme or pun
That's my way of having fun
I dream of things odd and flighty
Like 'saddle bags' on Aphrodite
Mister Bond with lispy speech
'Sacred cows' I love to breach

To tease, jest and deceive
Having something 'up my sleeve'
Is how I like to spend my days
Give it a spin...see how it plays

A staid remark, made by some
Fodder for me, it can become
A clever comment, right on cue
Ahh, another jocular coup

It's fun to watch bewildered faces
As my comedic mind, goes
through its paces
To hear them groan, or see them blush
I must admit, is quite a rush

Sometimes, I'll let my friends deliver
A quip - And be the punchline giver
There's the same amount of levity
And lets them think, the joke's on me

This ploy's designed, to loosen up
The disheartened, and 'fill their cup'
If they crack a smile, I daresay
It may help to make their day

But some don't like my off-beat humor
I hear, "perhaps he has a tumor"
They say, I march to a different drummer
And all my jokes, are dumb and dumber

Critics - And I have a few
Are entitled to their point of view
But if they have no 'funny bone'
The fault is theirs, and theirs alone

Though, many do appreciate
My arid wit - Innate
They like the way I tell a joke
I'm at my best, when 'blowing smoke'

There are times, I do get burned
When humility has returned
But successes far outweigh
The 'pipers', which I have to pay

The dawn has brought a silv'ry morn
I've been up all night, 'popping corn'
Material - A brand-new batch-
To incubate, and watch them hatch

Humor as the 'staff of-life'-
Can heal the sick, and conquer strife
So, add this to my epitaph
"He amused us all, and made us laugh"

Everything To Gain

I was once, her greatest love
Her knight in shining steel
We would share our very souls
There was nothing we'd conceal

We spent each new day, lost in love
Our nights, enwrapped in bliss
The planning of our lives, ahead
Of the past, we'd reminisce

I held the future, in my arms
With everything to gain
I could barely comprehend
The heights we could attain

She was love, personified
Heaven's entryway
I thanked God, for molding her
Each and every day

I felt, someday, I'd surely wed
The woman of my dreams
Then, one day, I broke her heart
It's over now, it seems

I recall her teary eyes
The look upon her face
I will lament, forever
My humbling fall from grace

A friend told her, I'd been untrue
For, she never did suspect
Now, my world, is upside down
What else did I expect?
I took the love, she freely gave
Her dignity and her pride
Dragged them through the depths...
I cheated and I lied

I hurt the only one I loved
For a cheap and tawdry thrill
I now regret, my errant ways
And they haunt me, still

Forgiveness, is my only hope
To absolve me of my sin
Though, if freed, could I be true
Or would I fail, again

Perhaps, the fate of one like me
Is fixed, and set in stone
I've done a cruel and wicked
deed For which, I can't atone

My fervent wish - My constant prayer
Will not be answered, 'til
That wondrous day, she says to me
"My dear, I love you, still."

Devastation

I had another tiff, today
They're happening all too often
My temper's ever on display
The dialog never seems to soften

People whom I once admired
Are beginning to desert me
I know in my heart, they've all conspired
To embarrass and to hurt me

I don't need them, at all, you see
These former friends of mine
Ever being at odds with me
And I'm sure, it's by design

Why are they tormenting me
With their vexing little remarks?
I can do without, this emotional debris
And the contention, that it sparks

I believe they're trying to drive me mad
Always putting me to the test
Controlling my mind, and may I add
With my ruin, they are obsessed

I'm in a state of total confusion
There is no longer, 'black or white'
Ever full of fear and disillusion
Such is my constant plight

If I am to remain quite sane
I must devise a scheme

To keep them out of my domain
And retain my self-esteem

I could always shut them out
And pretend they don't exist
I'd no longer have to rail and shout
Shake and bang my fist

If that would be the case
I could face the world, undaunted
Though, avoidance could hardly erase
The visions, with which I'm haunted

I see their faces, everywhere
(How they like to tease)
With hollow eyes - A relentless stare
That brings me to my knees

Their voices, too, I can't escape
They're baiting me, for sure
My very soul, they're about to rape
More, I can't endure

Alas, I feel I must retreat
To my own little 'ivory tower'
Free from torment and deceit
A security-laden bower

Maybe then, it all will stop
Or subside a bit, at least
From my brow, the sweat, I'd mop
Then, I'd be released-

From this curse, that's taken its toll
On my sanity and my pride
Much of my life, it has stole
Leaving me 'flogged' and 'crucified'

My spirit, they can never kill
Nor, commandeer my life
I'll take it first - I swear I will
By tablet, gun or knife

Then, my friend, it will all cease
This long and bumpy ride
At last, I'll find eternal peace
With God, I will abide

Quickly now, I must not tarry
Lest I lose my nerve
And be an incessant adversary
To these demons, that I serve

God, forgive me, what I do
But this urge, I must obey
Soon, I'll be coming home to You
So Lord, prepare the way

But if you feel I do not merit
To view You, in Your glory
See your kingdom, and to share it
Toward your servant, be conciliatory

As I am soon about to expire
(Your wretched, unworthy son)
I pray, I can escape the fire
But my God, let Your will be done

The Breaching

A fickle master, is the heart
Tough as nails, then breaks apart
For every notion
A new emotion-
Will arrive, and then depart

So hard, it can't be reached
Of a heart, it's often preached
All doubt, erase
Let's cut-to-the-chase
There's not one that can't be breached

I've seen hearts of flint
Tempered with just a hint
Of feminine sighs
And flirting eyes
That emit that special glint

My heart was once so dense
Unable to receive or dispense
A measure of feeling
Laying bare, and revealing
A core of impotence

I recall, there was a time
When I thought it was a crime
To alter my style
(I'd seldom smile)
There was no reason or rhyme

Though it was often scary
Being solitary
I preferred the seclusion
From the world's disillusion
I'd rather be aloof and contrary

Then one day, I met a man
And very soon, a rapport began
An affable fellow
With voice, so mellow
...Said he had a better plan

Attracted by his gaze
I hung on every phrase-
That flowed from his lips
Like nectar drips
And touched me, in many ways

From the very start
Loving thoughts, did he impart
Be humble and meek
Turn the other cheek
And harden not, your heart

His words, I could not ignore
And this fervent vow, I swore
That from my neck, I'd toss
This lumbering albatross-
Of strife —for now, and evermore

Over time, my views have altered
From my pledge, I have not faltered
I've slowed my descent
No longer, hell-bent
My demons, have all been haltered

We'll talk again, you see
This nameless man, and me
"Are you David or Sam?"
He said only, "I AM"
No! — It couldn't be!

Sanguine Reconciliation

Now that our friendship is waning
And our emotions, are constantly draining
It's time, I suspect
To take stock, and reflect
On whatever we may have remaining

We both have compassion to spare
But since our affinity is in disrepair
We must swallow our pride
So that love can abide
I will do my part - I swear

Though favors, I ever did strew
Carnality, was never the issue
Just a cohesive bond
In this life, and beyond
Anxiety, I never did wish you

I realize I've been obsessive
And yes, a little over-aggressive
But my intentions, dear lady
Were never the least bit shady
Though my behavior, you
found unimpressive

There was often no correlation
Between us, in our situation
Though our signals oft were crossed
I pray, all is not lost
And we still have a firm foundation

Since we've been estranged, my dear
No more sweet songs, do I hear
But the deafening tone
Of taps being blown
Resounding methodically in my ear

To my most recent pernicious infraction
I can understand your livid reaction
Yet, I pray, the healing will start
And save your poor heart-
A lifetime of perpetual traction

To memories, we will have to cling
Though, vestiges can hardly bring
The complete satisfaction
Of friendly interaction
Between a queen, and her jester king

I'm sure, we both feel remorse
That we couldn't stay the course
Though, we once had prosperity
These days, it's a rarity
And my vanity, is the source

Dear, each and every day
Our emotions came into play
We laughed and we cried
And I'm sure we both tried
To make it work - each in our own way

To avoid this carnage of our hearts
We must combine our mutual 'smarts'
An affable solution
Without retribution-
Must be paramount, on both our parts

If we can reach a joint accord
Our hearts will forever be moored
To the harbor of humility
Amidst the sea of tranquility
Blessed and sanctioned by the Lord

Flaxen Princess

My dear, when you are close to me
And we do intertwine
I know not what to say to thee
Oh, if a poet's tongue were mine

I'd find some clever words, you see
That are so very apt
To affirm, dear, what you mean to me
Your soul, for to enrapt

I would put them to the pen
When e'er I felt the need
To pull you close to me, and then
On my passion you could feed

A passion fueled, by each tender kiss
My spirits, you cause to leaven
A feeling, dear, such as this
Must surely come from Heaven

Dear, an aura of sanctity
Surrounds each flaxen tress
You could not mean more to me
My darling, may God bless

Life 101

Lovers come...lovers go
It's an ageless story
The pleasing lilt of her, "hello"
Those parting words, "I'm sorry"

Days and nights, fraught with bliss
The flames, that will be lit-
Can mask the perils of times like this
For, the bottom, you may hit

Once, I shouldered all the blame
If jilted by a lover
On my sleeve, I'd wear my shame
Dodge, and run for cover

I would feel, less a man
If a woman disavowed me
Deceived by some malicious plan
In self-pity, it would shroud me

When friends would say, I must forget
And leave it all behind
I would think them utter fools — and yet
They were only being kind

Over time, I've come to learn
The merit of this advice
Before I 'fall', I must discern
And consider the sacrifice

If a lover, now scoffs at me
I won't let it breach my skin
I must endure the test, you see
And not 'take it on the chin'

No longer do I feel abashed
When my manhood takes a hit
My eyes aren't wet...teeth aren't gnashed
To melancholy, I won't commit

I now say this, to all the men-
Who may follow in my shoes
If you feel used, now and then
You need not 'sing the blues'

If she tells you, that it's over —think
Perhaps it's not on you
From her cutting words, do not shrink
Consider it a fortuitous coup

Sun

The sun feels warm, upon my skin
Bespeaking the healing power within
By its soothing rays, we are gently kissed
As petals are, by the morning mist

With its radiant warmth, it has maintained
Life one earth - As God ordained
He's fixed it there, since the dawning
To sustain the existence, that was spawning

For millennia, we have revered this star
Viewing its magnificence, from afar
A daily vigil, since man's creation
And will be still, for the duration

It's ever been there - This celestial giant
Imposing, and comletely self-reliant
Spewing forth, its torrid gases
Emitting its warmth, to the terrestrial masses

This flaming orb, we take for granted
Won't be altered, or supplanted
Though, when its fiery breath, is at last withdrawn
All will perish - The king and the pawn

The Essence of My Being

Kindly words...a gentle touch
I ever try to impart
Niceties, I share with you
That come straight from the heart

I seek no gain no recompense
For what I say or do
I give to you, because I care
Each act, I swear, is true

Compassion is my driving force
More precious than a jewel
I employ it, each and everyday
And uphold the 'golden rule'

If I am wronged, I feel no rage
But try to reconcile
Vengeance, I will never use
Meeting bitterness with a smile

Perhaps you think, I put on airs
My manner, but a ruse
Meant only for effect
To deceive and confuse

I can't blame your skeptic mind
For thinking me a fraud
With the world today, as it is
Full of viciousness and gaud-

It's easy to expect the worst
When the best, is seldom seen

Where, many people go through life
With hearts and souls, unclean

Life's too short for rivalry
Contention only breeds scorn
There are some, who will not show love
For such as these, I mourn

I can't live my life that way
With nerves all taut and stressed Instead,
I think of ethereal things
They soothe, and give me rest

Fervent love, is a panacea
The most that one can give
I let it Saturate my heart
Then empty, as through a sieve

Drenching everyone I meet-
With the essence of my being
Then show them all, the gentleness
Of this person, they are seeing

I'll wear humanity as my crown
As long as I'm on earth
Bringing peace and joy to everyone
And ampleness of mirth

Amid the dark, I'll be a light
For everyone to see
I'll glorify and emulate
The man from Galilee

There are some that chide me
For being a 'pollyanna'
I smile, and give credit to
My daily dose of 'manna'

Given me by my God
(This food I will not hoard)
But let it flow from me to you
'Til we're all of one accord

If I can get you on my side
'Fore the world intervenes
I will do whate're it takes
The end justifies the means

So when you,re sad, and need a friend
Nothing, I will spare
I'll impart to you, my special gift
Laughter, and a prayer

If what from me, you do receive
(As I do freely give it)
You take into your heart and soul
Then go, my friend, and live it

Friends Parting

When you go, you'll leave behind
This flame, which you have lit
It's burning, still, in my heart and mind
But, I'll get over it

Those cute bandanas that you wore
The way they neatly fit
I will enjoy them, no more
But, I'll get over it

Gone, too, will be that winning smile
That never seemed to quit
I'd drink it in, all the while
But, I'll get over it

When you'd glide 'cross the floor
I swear, I'd see angels flit
Around your face and hands, and more
But, I'll get over it

When I see that empty chair
Where you used to sit
I think of all the words we'd share
But, I'll get over it

Our special love, was so sublime
I really must admit
It truly transcended space and time
But, I'll get over it

This void, you left, within my heart
Is now, a gaping pit
Now, is when the heartaches start
But, I'll get over it

Dear, myself, you did imbue
With every benefit
Now, is when the tears ensue
But, I'll get over it

When I leave this place, for to die
I won't lament, a bit
For I'll meet you, dear, up in the sky
THEN, I'll get over it

New Millennium Resolutions

As I begin this solemn versing
There are some thoughts,
I've been rehearsing
They are for us, the children of God
May He give this poem, an approving nod

With regards, this new
'Brotherhood of Man'
Let me not merely, do what I can
I solemnly pledge, for all our sakes
That I will do, whatever it takes

May love and peace, in your
heart, be teeming
And that smile, on your
face, keep beaming
I pray, in contentment, your
soul will abound
And with happiness, few
people have found

The only way to achieve these ends
Is to, with everyone, make amends
Bury your resentment, pique and ire
Toward harmony, you should aspire

If, with a friend, you form a rift
Please, don't give then 'short shrift'
A reconciliation, should be your desire
Lest the circumstances, become dire

If enmity from your mind, can be lifted
Consider yourself extremely gifted
My friend, if you can do this

It will surely secure eternal bliss

Smile at everyone you see
What a happy lot they'll be
Call them all by their names
The gentlemen and the dames

Friend, I'm trying not to preach to you
With a helping hand, I reach to you
You harbor some demons, as do we all
That makes us, at times, stumble and fall

Life can be cruel and unforgiving
At times, we may wonder,
why we are living
Our hopes and dreams, it oft times dashes
But like a phoenix, we can
rise from the ashes

Emerge more radiant, than ever before
Ready to meet, what the world has in store
Let's vow jointly, to do whatever it takes
To rid our minds, of sorrow and aches

Now, as we enter a new millennium
I pray, your heart won't
swing like a pendulum
Never at rest, as the ocean's foam
Or the perpetual motion, of a metronome

But steady and true, never to falter
The budding debut, of a virtual 'Gibraltar'
Friend, I pray you can stay on course
Never putting the cart, before the horse

We all could be much better persons
Save, for the character in us, that worsens
Whenever we utter a disparaging word
Toward one of our brethren,
for to be heard

A word that cuts, just like a blade
Leaving a wound, that's openly laid
The breach may heal, but leave a scar
And their self-esteem, severely mar

Once a word is spoken, it
can't be recovered
This, I have many times, discovered
So soften your words, and
make no mistake
With a loose word, their
spirit, you may break

Stroke someone's ego, yours it won't harm
Their marked anxiety, it may disarm
Say they look nice, when they don't
You think it may hurt, but it won't

They say, you have no sense of humor
I hope, my friend, this is just a rumor
We must laugh at the world,
and all its vices
Or in our lives, there may be a crisis

To laugh at ourselves, is essential
If we are to reach, our full potential
It's vital to temper reverence with frivolity
Or it can lead to self-idolatry

Remember well, how I've spoken
Take a deep breath, and come out smokin
Try not to judge and ridicule
My friend, just heed the 'golden rule'

If this rule, you'll take to heart
Virulence, you will outsmart
So, live your life, as it was meant to be
Spirit and mind, completely free

Forbidden Love

I write these lines, and as I do
Tears may stain the pages
Nevermore, can I be with you
For my sins, those are the wages

I avowed my love, right from the start
As long as we should live
To you, I gave my eager heart
But alas, it was not mine to give

Another woman shares my world
With a commitment, ever binding
The web of deceit, has around me, curled
And it strangles me - I'm finding

My true feelings, I must bring to light
I can keep them in, no more
I will now do what is right
Confess, and close the door

Those honeyed words, I would choose
To fill your lovely head
Was the ploy that I would use
To seek and gain your bed

I thought of you, as a tart
The flame of love, I'd douse
Dear, I toyed with your heart
As a cat does, with a mouse

In this evil man, you placed your trust
With the candor of a child
But my intent, was merely lust
Your honor, I defiled

I've hurt you, dear - forgive me, please
The way I led you on
The guilt, has brought me to my knees
My sweet and gentle swan

I pray, someday, you'll find a man
Whose heart, is not like mine
Filled with a cold and devious plan
Rather - virtuous and benign

As for me, I'll try to deal
With the pain, that I have wrought
God knows, the remorse I feel
A hard lesson to be taught

Though, the grass may be a brighter green
On someone else's block
You may find yourself between
A hard place, and a rock

A Blessing In Disguise

People curse the rainy day
They say, "I want it sunny"
To hear them carry on that way
You know, it's almost funny

Don't they know, a rainy day
Can be a blessing in disguise?
Trying to hold the clouds at bay
Wouldn't be so very wise

The rain, is but an interlude
Between two sunny days
Its time is brief — and I conclude
It helps in many ways

The rain has therapeutic worth
As it falls upon the land
Without it, planet Earth-
Is a pile of scorching sand

There are some obvious benefits
Imparted by a shower
It 'greens' the land, and transmits
Animation to a flower

A rainy day, has this effect
But this is only part
It gives one time to reflect
On matters of the heart

When e'er the day, is damp and drear
You'll find, your mind has wandered
To family and friends, that you revere
And occasions that you've squandered

Call a friend, which you haven't seen
Because, you never had the time
Imagine, what a call from you can mean
Go ahead — invest a dime

Remind your family, of your love
Have a heart-to-heart connection
The rain can be a gentle shove
To a friendship resurrection

Be grateful, too, that you are sound
In body, and in mind
That you're not six-feet under ground
Constricted and confined

As long as there's a breath to take
There is time to make amends
If a compassionate life, you don't forsake
You'll be rewarded, when it ends

So, when those clouds, begin to form
And that sunny window closes
Disregard the impending storm
Stop, and smell the roses

117

Change of Heart

In the spring, 'neath April skies
All looks new, through a young man's eyes
The grass below - The sun above
And in his heart, he dreams of love

Though, being young, he may not feel
True love's warmth...its fond appeal
Seeing the world, through eyes so blind
He may choose the other kind

Not a fervent love, but one contrasting
Transient - Not everlasting
Using youthful wit and guile
To serve his ego, for awhile

To this life, I can relate
A roguish air — A swaggering gait
Making love, was just a game
No emotion felt - No heart aflame

Every day, life was grand
A different girl, would hold my hand
No thought was given, to have just one
Variety, was too much fun

They say that everyone, has a match
But it comes with strings - There's a catch
You must be honest, loyal and true
With hearts as one - No longer two

This view was nice, but not for me
To commit, was not my destiny
I'd be a cad, and 'play the field'
To the domestic life, I'd never yield

I swore, I'd never give my heart
To see it broken, and torn apart
Play it straight - Don't take a chance
Why alter my present circumstance?

No one had ever turned my head
I kept it firmly attached, instead
'Til a girl, with a raven tress
Caused my heart to acquiesce

My priorities, I've now rearranged
Heart and mind...no longer estranged
My every thought, is of her
I am in love - If you prefer

With songs of joy, my heart resounds
As my love grows, by leaps and bounds
A love to stand the 'test of time'
Never to falter, but forever climb

If in my life, she'll always stay
Loneliness, will be kept at bay
Likewise, gloom and wanderlust
For, with her, my heart, I will entrust

So, I'll live 'happily ever after'
Seeing her smile...hearing her laughter
I'll praise the lord, all my life
For this lovely girl, who's now my wife

Ode To A Straw

A thin cylindrical piece of plastic
It can be stiff and rigid, or elastic
A simple little gadget — beats all I ever saw
We couldn't do without you, you simple little straw

You're hollow in the middle, all the way through
An adult or a kid'll, make equal use of you
That's the wonder of you; you're a modest little tool
Even a child can use you; you're so cool

They inhale through you, and up comes the draught
The entire length, of your resinous shaft
You provide a means, for our bodies to be sated
For our thirsts, to be completely subjugated

If a concoction's too thick, you may collapse
And thus be discarded - well, perhaps
There can be a use for anything, even if it's busted
If you proclaim it loud enough, upon the public, it can be thrusted

All one has to do, is use their imagination
And anything's possible, if you show the inclination
Don't ask me what it can be, it's up to you
But I would like to see, the conclusion that you drew

Another use for a defective straw
Is to attack someone, who 'sticks in your craw'
You just fill the chamber, with your own guided missile
And watch it hit its mark, slicker than a whistle

You're multi-talented, you piece of polymer, you
Singing your praises, is long overdue
In the hollow tube realm, there aren't many cuter
You're a liquid inhaler, and a lethal peashooter

119

The Fickle Mind

We had a few years
A very good run
But it now appears It's all but done

Not that I didn't have a clue-
That each day, could be our last
With every passing hour, I knew
The end was coming fast

At times, the things you'd do and say
Would be completely off-the-wall
What message you'd try to convey
Dear, would be anybody's call

I recall, the friendly words you spoke
Every one — really
And now I fear, you were 'blowing smoke'
And I was inhaling, freely

You'd hug my neck...kiss my cheek
And tell me, that you love me
Our ardent love, was at its peak
Next day, away, you'd shove me

I can't forget your lying tongue
How it cut me, deep
Still, to you, I always clung
Though it hurt, and made me weep

Even though, you'd break my heart
And leave me sad and teary-
If in my life, you were not a part
It would be so very dreary

Although, at times, you'd play the shrew
And angry words, recite
My regrets of knowing you
Have been so very slight

I thank you for the talks we had
The trifling and the deep
Is there remorse? Yes, a tad
But those memories, I'll ever keep

If I brought some laughter to your heart
(Weaving sunshine, from the rain)
Then I can smile, as I depart
Knowing, all was not in vain

I've come away with mixed emotions
Though, my heart's still on my sleeve
A head filled, with bewildering notions
Of friendship, I can't retrieve

If this is to be our last hurrah
(A bitter pill to swallow)
Despite every glaring faux pas-
Each vow, deceitful and hollow-

You left your mark, upon my soul
I'll give you that, at least
But were you pixie or troll
Beauty, or the beast

About the Author

HELLO, MY NAME IS LLOYD ANDRESEN
I STARTED COMPOSING IN THE LATE '90S.
IT WAS NEVER MY PASSION NOR MY DREAM
TO WRITE POETRY, BUT A FRIEND ASKED ME
TO WRITE A POEM FOR HER BIRTHDAY. I JOTTED
DOWN A FEW LINES AND GAVE IT TO HER.
LATER, SHE THANKED ME, AND TOLD OF HOW IT
MADE HER CRY. IT WAS THEN I REALIZED THAT PERHAPS
I HAD A MODICUM OF TALENT FOR WRITING.
BESIDES THE SELECTIONS YOU ARE ABOUT TO PERUSE,
I HAVE WRITTEN FOR FAMILY AND FRIENDS.
THANK YOU FOR SHOWING INTEREST IN MY BOOK,
AND I HOPE YOU FIND IT ENTERTAINING.

SINCERELY,
LLOYD ANDRESEN

Printed in the United States
By Bookmasters